THE WRITER'S WORKOUT BOOK

113 STRETCHES TOWARD BETTER PROSE

ART PETERSON

Berkeley
National Writing Project
1996

Please direct reprinting requests and book orders to:

National Writing Project
5511 Tolman Hall
University of California
Berkeley, CA 94720-1670

Telephone 510-642-0963
Fax 510-642-4545

Library of Congress Cataloging-in-Publication Data

Peterson, Art.
    The writer's workout book: 113 stretches toward better prose / Art Peterson.
        p. cm.
    ISBN 1-883920-11-6
    1. English language—Composition and exercises—Study and teaching (Sec-
ondary)—United States—Problems, exercises, etc. 2. Creative writing (Secondary
education)—United States—Problems, exercises, etc. I. Title.
LB1631.P446 1996
808'.042'0712—dc20
                                                                                96-7329
                                                                                CIP

Design and Layout: Paul Molinelli
Cover Design: William Peterson
Editor: Jane Juska

ACKNOWLEDGMENTS

The summer I started this book was the summer the hamster died. This little tragedy was only one of the mishaps that befell us during a housesitting experience thirteen years ago. Exotic plants expired. The garbage disposal disintegrated. A cup of coffee seemed to jump from my hand, its contents staining irreparably an expensive white sofa. Every day it was something else.

Perhaps the sensible thing to do would have been to call an exorcist, but instead I retreated to the wood-paneled study of this attractive (if rapidly deteriorating) suburban home and considered how I might bring a little order to my life. Rather than struggle with the poltergeist (or whatever was at hand), I looked forward to the upcoming school year, thinking hard about the patterns that had worked for me as a teacher of writing. What could I do to hold on to the spontaneity that makes for good teaching while reducing the one-damn-thing-after-another pressures that were part of the teaching life?

The Writer's Workout Book is the result of what started with those halting attempts. My partner and advisor in this effort has been my wife, Norma, herself a writer. She has worked hard to purge this book of tendencies toward textbook tone, pedantic authority, self-serving indulgence, romantic theorizing and educational cant. Her favorite critique, "I like some parts better than others," has been her way of encouraging me before we have settled down to some rewarding talk about revising the "others." I could not have written this book without her.

The other person who has made this book possible is Jim Gray, founder and former executive director of the National Writing Project. As he explains here in his preface, he decided *The Writer's Workout Book* should be published after I sent him what appears to me in retrospect a pretty raggedy draft. But Jim's influence on this book goes beyond his decision to see it published. He is the colleague more than any other who made me realize that I had ideas worth sharing with other teachers. He first bestowed on me this massive dose of self-confidence when, in 1981, I was invited to the Bay Area Writing Project (BAWP) summer institute. I returned to my classroom with a spring in my step. Now, many years later, I realize that I was one of hundreds of teachers he had helped in just this way.

Some others who need to be recognized:

- Jane Juska, my BAWP colleague and editor. Her good sense, refined ear and sharp humor very much helped shape this work.

- Mary Ann Smith and the late Miriam Ylvisaker who gave me encouragement as I began my revisions.

- Don Gallehr who read the book carefully and made a number of insightful suggestions, many of which I have incorporated.

- My brother, William Peterson, who created a cover totally in keeping with the playful tone I have attempted in this book.

- Paul Molinelli, our chief cook and bottle-washer of book production, who has brought to this project his abilities as a talented book designer and a demon proofreader.

- Diane (The Dickensian) Johnson.

- And finally my students, hundreds of them. A few of them are profiled here. The writing of some of them appears and is duly recognized. But many others have faced with good humor the primitive beginnings of the workouts that appear in this book. Their comments, while sometimes blunt, have almost always been useful. Every author should have the privilege of presenting his material to thirty sixteen-year-olds twenty minutes before lunchtime. After that the *Times Literary Supplement?* Hey, piece of cake.

CONTENTS

PREFACE

In *The Writer's Workout Book,* Art Peterson has created a resource for teachers who enjoy the give and take of teaching writing and want to know more about what students can be taught about the craft. These 113 lessons sample much of what Art has found to be important in his own teaching of writing over a distinguished thirty-two-year career in the San Francisco public schools. For much of this time, Art has known and practiced the important approaches to the teaching of writing that have surfaced during the lifetime of the National Writing Project.

However, he has never been wedded to any one right way to teach writing. And this, more than anything else, probably accounts for the success he has had as a teacher. He is not a zealot. Rather, he has been open to whatever works. In particular, he is one of those teachers who is fascinated by the nuts and bolts of writing, and it is this interest which has inspired the lessons in this book. These "workouts" will lead students to think like writers, observing and recording the world, putting their memories to work, developing and organizing ideas, structuring logical arguments in varied forms, connecting with readers and manipulating sentences. Young writers as well as their teachers will emerge from these workouts with an increased respect for the power of words and a greater relish for the joy of playing with language.

Art is a great teacher, and he has been widely recognized as such. Sarah Freedman, Director of the Center for Writing and Literacy at U.C. Berkeley, chose Art's classroom for the research that led to her book, *Response to Student Writing.* His work has been profiled in the *Los Angeles Times* and in the *San Francisco Examiner.* In 1991, the year of his retirement, Art was recognized by the English-Speaking Union for having had six of his students, over the years, as grand prize winners in the Union's annual essay contest. Art is a writer as well as a teacher, having published over fifty articles and other education-related materials as well as three humor books.

As a natural humorist, he has succeeded in teaching, in part, because he has refused to take the serious work of teaching and learning too seriously. Both the lessons and the essays in *The Writer's Workout Book* are laced with a whimsy and irony that make it a constant joy to read. Many teachers know Art's work through his best-selling and hilarious book on teaching—*Teachers: A Survival Guide for the Grown Up in the Classroom,* (New American Library, 1985). I predict, however, that once teachers see the range, potential, and practicality of the many specific lessons in *The Writer's Workout Book,* this will become his most popular and certainly most used work.

The publication history of *The Writer's Workout Book* is somewhat complicated. When Art retired from the San Francisco schools, the district office immediately hired him as a curriculum consultant, and it was during this period that he wrote the first draft of this book for use by his fellow San Francisco teachers. When this draft was printed, Art sent me a copy, and I was enchanted. I remember reading aloud sections to my colleague, Mary Ann Smith, that had us both roaring with laughter. I called Art and told him that this was a book that I thought the Writing Project should publish and asked him to send a copy to Miriam Ylvisaker, who at that time was the National Writing Project editor. Miriam also fell in love with the book and worked with Art on an expansion of the early draft; that revision, after being reviewed, was accepted by Miriam before she died. The book had not been printed by the time Richard Sterling took over as executive director, so Richard, after having the book reviewed once again, accepted *The Writer's Workout Book* for publication.

When Miriam Ylvisaker died, it was a terrible loss for the National Writing Project. Miriam was beloved and respected by all who had known and worked with her. She was bright and principled and a magnificent editor, and it was Art Peterson who was the unanimous first choice to replace her.

—*Jim Gray, former executive director, National Writing Project*

INTRODUCTION: WHAT WRITERS DO

I have a warm spot in my heart for used lesson plans. Along with unspent lire and the keys to a long-gone Dodge Dart, these documents have made it to the "Someday This Stuff Will Come In Handy" corner of my basement. Now, I have had the opportunity to burrow through years of personal classroom history, sorting out the inspired ideas and good tries from the false starts and bad judgments. Out of this rummaging, I've created 113 writing workouts to help students, and especially teachers, think about the small steps writers take as they learn their craft.

I say especially teachers because I suspect I am not the only teacher who has felt uneasy teaching "Writing." For me, what writers do has always seemed kind of artsy and exotic. The writer's life was a big jump from the tenured and bureaucratic existence to which I had submitted myself. I was too (blush) normal to know much about writing. I had been neither On the Road nor Over the Cuckoo's Nest. The black dogs of depression that drove Franz Kafka to great literature had seldom intruded on the core optimism which allowed me to thrive as a teacher. Sure, I had been a writer, but mostly a writer of "curriculum guides." I ask you, would Norman Mailer be caught dead writing a curriculum guide?

These were my insecurities when I was invited to spend five weeks one summer as a teacher-consultant with the Bay Area Writing Project. I am not going to tell you that this experience—with its requirement that the participants write—awakened some inner muse and unsealed a vein of talent I did not know I had. No. Rather, I began to wonder if talent wasn't—well—overrated. Working through many revisions, I came to believe what the ads from the Famous Writers' School had been telling me all along: writing can, indeed, be learned.

Even more importantly, I came to see that as a teacher of writing, my job was not to scout out fledgling candidates for some future Book

Critics' Circle Award, but rather to use writing to help all students learn to think, including—maybe even especially—those students who, in their lives, will write very little. I saw that the future waitpersons, stockbrokers, and garage mechanics in my class needed the writer's ability to generate, develop, organize, alter, and evaluate ideas just as much as the student who would someday take a shot at the Great American Novel.

From then on my job as a teacher became to isolate, teach, and connect the practical attitudes and skills which would help my students act like writers. I began to think of writing as The Basic Skill, essential not only for the bookish kids who were already trying out reasonable facsimiles of Sylvia Plath, but also for those students who would someday argue with a landlord, tell a joke, or court a lover. So just what is it that writers do that we should all be doing?

I. Writers Speak Up

H. L. Mencken once described writing for a living as a kind of personality disorder: "(The writer's) overpowering impulse is to gyrate before his fellow men, flapping his wings and emitting defiant yells. This being forbidden by the police, he yells on paper. Such is the thing called self-expression."

I have no doubt that, on many a Saturday night, any number of the students I have taught have carried on vigorously in the manner Mencken describes. Monday morning, however, is a different story. How do we nudge students to flap their arms on paper, to have confidence that their experience is worth gyrating about?

As a teacher of writing, I have spent many hours prodding students into believing in the importance of sharing what is unique about them.

"Why don't you write about that?" I ask an American-born Korean girl who is describing the fights which occur between her and her immigrant mother each time the girl wants to wear white—a color associated with death in Korean culture. "Why would anyone else care?" she wonders.

"I don't think it's very interesting," demurs the babysitter who, in an essay, has just exposed in ironic detail the hyper-rigid child-rearing practices of the sixties radical for whom she babysits. When I tell her that some people would pay for this information, she allows herself a slight smile. The workouts in Part I of this book are intended to help novice writers such as these develop confidence in the value of their experience.

II. Writers Pay Attention

The writing classroom is not the place for a test every Friday. Whatever seeds are sown cannot be harvested at weekly intervals. Indeed, they may sprout and blossom only years later.

I was reminded of this understanding when I ran across an "average" student of several years previous who had just seen soon-to-be Vice-President Al Gore up close.

"His hands don't fit his body," she said. "He's got these fingers that start thick and grow thin at the ends. He's a big guy and he is always moving these delicate hands around as he talks. It makes him seem pretty sensitive for a jock type."

I wanted to change her grade. The woman had learned—alas, maybe not from me—what I was trying to teach: She was paying attention.

While students are in my class, I want them to learn to take in everything, a habit I try to model. I believe I lead a richer life because I've learned to see like a writer. I am addicted to noticing both the trivial—the principal's socks that don't quite match today—and the important—the tough kid who winces ever so slightly as I read aloud a Karl Shapiro poem, demonstrating that maybe he is not as immune to the power of poetry as he claims.

Part II of *The Writer's Workout Book* presents challenges to sharpen observation skills.

III. Writers Think First

In a culture in which a "dialogue" is often composed of advocates and critics of cross-dressing yelling at each other between commercials on *Sally!*, writers provide an anchor of reasonableness. Writers—at least good writers—don't jabber or blurt. They organize their minds. They provide models that convince even when they irritate.

When we sign on as teachers, we commit ourselves to battling nonsense. I can't say my classroom has always been a bastion of orderly thought, but when a colleague told me, somewhat disapprovingly, that students came out of my class "pretty left brainy," I took this remark as a compliment.

When I have thought about my teaching goals, I have sometimes conceived a scenario in which, maybe ten years into the future, any one of the thousands of students who have been through my classroom will, one night, unable to sleep, flick on a late-night radio call-in show and hear someone speaking in hushed tones of suppressed cancer cures or of scientists who have met mysterious deaths after designing automobiles that run on mineral water or of the first American moon landing that was, says the caller, a mirror trick. And the former student will ask the darkness: "Says who?"

The workouts in Part III of this book promote the power of logical argument.

IV. Writers Consider Other People

Teachers and students spend a lot of time feeling each other out, looking for ways to connect. They need to be, as they say in the writing texts, "aware of their audiences."

Having some sense of the teacher as audience, a student is not likely to respond to an essay question with sentences like "Desdemona, she burst fresh out of sight." A teacher, on the other hand, needs to communicate in language that takes into account the values, knowledge, and tastes of her students without resorting to quoting from the latest issue of *Sassy* magazine. The writing classroom provides a dicey, if instructive, laboratory for communication that considers others.

The workouts in Part IV present ways for writers to connect with an audience.

V. Writers Create Choices

Most students come to writing class reluctant to pursue the possibilities that working writers take for granted. This may be because they have learned to be very nervous about "whoing" when they should been "whoming" and the like. These fears limit their willingness to take chances. I have taught many students who, if they were quarterbacks and I the coach, would want me to script, not just the first ten plays, but the entire game regardless of what happens on the field.

So even as I am committed to structured learning, I often have quoted Thomas Edison: "There ain't no rules here; we're trying to get something done."

I want students to understand that a command of rhetoric opens up worlds of precise nouns and power verbs, accurate comparisons and imagined scenarios, simple sentences and baroque paragraphs.

I have spent much of my career trying to convince students that just because they are writing for school, they do not have a responsibility to be boring. Yes, I tell the student bogged down in a generic "report" on the Golden Gate Bridge, it's OK to tell about how, as a young boy at the bridge's fiftieth anniversary celebration, he thought he was going to die—crushed to death or drowned as he was stuck in a gridlock of thousands of older and taller people, inching across the perilously swaying span. Yes, he could do that and also make sure we knew that the bridge was a "symmetrical cantilevered suspension" engineered by Joseph Strauss and opened on April 28, 1937.

Another time, a student presented a precise but pedantic analysis of the Matisse painting *Femme au Chapeau*, one of the jewels in the collection of the San Francisco Museum of Modern Art.

"So," I asked, "what is it that attracts you to the museum?"

"You meet a better class of men there," she said.

Her next draft kept the analysis but was a lot more interesting.

The workouts in Part V explore the rhetorical choices available to writers.

VI. Writers Love Words

I'll admit that, to the uninitiated, the little rush of joy that comes over a writer when, in revision, "natty" replaces "neat," may seem an over-refined pleasure, like the thrill the fox hunter feels when the hounds pick up the scent. But as a teacher of writing, my job is to create language addicts, to load students up with words that connote anger or humor, that establish sympathy or sarcasm.

I remember a girl discussing her college essay with me. She was a flute player applying to a prestigious music department. I asked if she played any instruments other than the flute.

"I used to play the ocarina," she said.

We were on to something. In the final draft of her essay, the word "ocarina" turned up at the beginning and at the end. How could an admissions officer resist this artful use of a lovely word? The girl was accepted. Later she wrote to say she was the leader of the only ocarina trio on campus. I wanted to think she wasn't joking.

The workouts in Part VI explore the pleasures and possibilities of words.

VII. Writers Keep Trying

As we will see, much advice about writing is paradoxical. The chief among these paradoxes may be that writing is both easy and difficult. On the one hand, because we all have language, writing comes naturally. We need only purchase a paisley-covered journal, a pen with the right colored ink, a cup of latte at a commodious cafe and settle down to uncork our personal reservoir of words and thoughts. This isn't me. For me, reading over my deeply felt first draft is often like waking from a dream in which I have performed lifesaving brain surgery only to realize I don't even know the difference between the cerebrum and the cerebellum.

I have had many students who write with more ease than I do. Still, I have worked to discourage the lackadaisical attitude which E. B. White satirizes in the doggerel: Sing ho, sing hey/ He thinks he'd like to write a play/ But only at certain times of day.

Natural is a start, but then comes the mixing and distilling, shrinking and expanding, tightening and loosening that is revision.

Unfortunately, when I mount my classroom soapbox preaching the need to keep reworking a piece, I sound rather like *McGuffey's Reader*, circa 1895: persistence, hard work, self-discipline pay off. The kids start drifting away, more because of my stridency than my sentiment. Sometimes I find it more effective to merely call attention to a remark by Thomas Mann: "A writer is someone for whom writing is harder than it is for other people."

The workouts in Part VII and elsewhere in this book help make the difficult work of revision, if not exactly fun, at least intellectually diverting.

Finally, a disclaimer to be read as if it were printed in red ink and capital letters: The workouts in this book are inspired by my lessons, but they are not intended to be your lessons. In thirty years I have collected wonderful ideas, large and small from hundreds of teachers, but I have never found an idea that could be transported intact to my classroom. Even my own lesson, fresh off the drawing board for first period, often needs to be rebuilt for second period. All curriculum that works is made in individual classrooms. I present these 113 workouts as a gift for teachers, who, like me, are inspired to create by reflecting on specific examples rather than general pronouncements. As you contemplate these teaching "recipes," I hope you will think of yourself not as a cook but as a chef.

PART I: WRITERS SPEAK UP

- Look, Ma, I'm Writing Prose:
  Five Subjects to Start You Writing

Diving In: The Importance of Writing on Day One

THE first day of school is often deceptively mellow. In the halls, voices murmur, lockers close gently with muffled thunks. I am seduced by the smell of fresh floor wax. The kids, in their new dos and pristine Reeboks, edge into the classroom as if arriving late for church. They sit erect and appear alert, respectful, optimistic—generic Good Kids. I think, "Hey, this is going to be easy."

No one warns me that the smiling girl with the orthodontically perfect teeth, acrylic nails, and retro-Farah Fawcett hair will soon submit obsessive journal entries detailing the slimy exploits of her allegedly two-timing boyfriend. "What would you do?" she will demand.

I don't yet know that the leather-packed boy in the last row, the one with the intelligent, intense eyes will soon turn hostile and unforgiving after I make an ill-considered sarcastic remark about his free form punctuation. But for now I haven't a clue. I am a little like the falling window washer as he plunges past the twenty-third floor, reporting, "So far, so good."

I am tempted to extend the good vibes by going with the flow: calling the roll slowly, diddling around with seating charts, soliciting applications for attendance monitor.

However, I also know that all the while, beneath this agreeable facade, terror lurks. The kids are thinking, "Here I am in a writing class and I don't know how to write." This is different from the doubts students may feel on the first day of, say, chemistry class. Chemistry is new, writing isn't. They have been writing mostly all their lives and can't help secretly wondering "So, what's my excuse?"

First day housekeeping chores—as we call them in the trade—will not answer these doubts. Better to put aside the class lists and begin the process of convincing students they know more than they think they do. On Day One, they need to write. But they should not write merely to generate a "writing sample," maybe the closest thing we have to an academic urine test. They should write to discover all over again they can do it.

What will they write about? At moments like this, I try to keep in mind an anecdote Writing Project old timers tell about Ed Allen, a legendary teacher-consultant.

"How many of you have trekked with Indians?" Ed would ask his students. Silence.

"How many of you have not wanted to get out of bed in the morning?" That's different. Ed makes the point that beginning writers write best about subjects they know.

But while students need to write of what they know and care about, it's also important to allow a little distance. This is a school, not a computer dating service. I've always felt uncomfortable asking a perfect stranger intimate questions like, "What is the greatest misconception about you?" (Maybe later, but not on Day One.) Also, I am looking for a topic which will generate conversation, not monologues; these thirty individuals need to become a class.

Here is a topic that works because it draws on shared memory. Ask students to recount an experience with a toy or game about which they have strong memories and feelings. Begin with some brainstorming, drawing out the names of classic playthings: PlayDoh, Crayola Crayons, Candyland games and Nerf Balls. The effect of generating such a list will be to encourage some students to write on the same topic.

On Day Two, students share their experiences. The conversation begins to turn a motley crew into a cohesive group.

Below are five more workouts intended to jog memories and encourage students to listen to their voices. Think of these workouts, as well as the others in this book, as etched in a substance closer to silly putty than to stone. They are yours to renovate, reshape, and otherwise make appropriate for your classroom.

Look, Ma, I'm Writing Prose:
Five Subjects to Start You Writing

1. Remember a Daydream

"Stop daydreaming," says the teacher. True, you can't learn much geography while fantasizing about your life as a movie star, but here's a chance to put your reverie to another use. Recall one of your daydreams. Keep running the story past your inner eye until you have brought the specifics into focus.

The example which follows probably won't read much like one of your daydreams. But it could come pretty close to one enjoyed by your mother or grandmother. Wandering minds are nothing new.

> *I remember thinking that when I grew up I would go to a nightclub every night. I would wear a strapless gown, and the gentleman would bring me an orchid corsage. We would sit at a little linen-covered table with a tiny shaded lamp, under artificial palms and a full paper moon, sipping tall sweet rum drinks with a pineapple wedge on the rim of the glass and a made-in-Japan paper umbrella popping out of it.*
>
> *And as we gaily laughed, the orchestra would strike up a mambo, and we'd head out to the dance floor of the Club Trocadero.*
> —Alice Kahn

2. Confess to the Attraction of a Former Bad Habit

Remember when every other word out of your mouth seemed to be "yo" or "way" or "fresh," and you couldn't seem to stop? Remember when you would feel the uncontrollable urge to eat chocolate or watch "The Young and the Restless" or go shopping for things you didn't need or talk to your friend for hours on the phone?

Write about your winning struggle against a minor vice you decided you could do without. What was its appeal? How did you kick the habit?

3. Reconstruct a Movie Moment

Recall a single movie scene that for you was so memorable it has eclipsed the rest of the film.

"Bambi" was full of darting butterflies and sleeping possums. Deer learned to walk in the snow and bunnies thumped their feet. Children see all this and most forget it as they grow older. But they remember the moment that Bambi's mother is shot. Find a similar moment in another film and recreate it in as much detail as you can.

4. Catalogue Your Friends and Acquaintances

Find an adjective that separates each of the people you know well from the others. Then write some sentences to prove that each deserves the label.

Example:
Pamela is the most health-obsessed person I know. Raised by a mother who considers french fries the nutritional equivalent of rat poison, Pamela's mind is a computer programmed to scan the ingredients of a can of minestrone, calculating the risk of colon cancer for a sixteen-year-old. I do not believe she owns a salt shaker or even any salt to shake. Others have cereal with milk and fruit for breakfast. Pamela has fiber with calcium and potassium.*

Try some adjectives which are a step beyond commonplace. Some starters: harried, feisty, affable, finicky, wholesome, bitter, pugnacious, youthful, testy, zealous, fearless, wacky, well-rested.

5. Recall the Story Behind a Possession

Look around for an object that brings back memories: a poster, a certificate of achievement, a baseball card, a valentine, a book, an old outfit you no longer wear, a photograph, a good luck charm, a letter you've kept. Replay the memories inspired by this object.

*Based on a column by Ellen Goodman

PART II: WRITERS PAY ATTENTION

- **How to See When You Look:**
  Four Ways to Pay Attention

- **Enlightenment for Beginners:**
  Three Ways to Use What You See

- **Bringing Out the Inner Eye:**
  Four Ways to Write from Memory

Vision Screening: Moving Beyond 20/20

I am dreaming. At the zoo, I see a student, standing in a group of maybe ten, staring into an empty cage. I approach. "This cage is empty," I say.

"Oh," she says, then moves on to the next empty cage and resumes staring.

I don't know what my unconscious is trying to tell me with this recurring weirdness, but recounting the dream in class, I put a didactic spin on it: the student is all of us who look but don't see. Often we make our mental movies with the lens cap off, but no film in the camera.

Teachers are not immune to lazy perception. I remember a midterm evaluation I received from a girl in the early 1980s.

"I think you are prejudiced against the boys who wear Wranglers," she wrote. Huh? As I had no idea what Wranglers were, I had to plead guilty. But I began to notice. There were Levis, there were Lees and there were Wranglers. And the Wranglers had not been handing in their homework. "So who's prejudiced?" I wondered. But, after that, the Wranglers got more attention.

By focusing on trousers, I learned about the teenage wardrobe-attitude connection, but what else might I be missing? With only one set of sensory equipment per customer, all observation is necessarily selective.

Here's a little assignment I use to make the point that what we see is what we focus on:

"Tonight we are going to watch TV, looking for a nominee in a new award category, Best Performance by an Extra. When you watch television dramas and movies on TV this evening, give your attention to the anonymous people in the background—the mothers scolding kids, the lovers sharing a sandwich in the park. Nominate a Best Extra, describing precisely his or her appearance and actions."

I warn students that they may not see much of some of these folks. A little creative padding may be necessary. In addition to providing a valuable lesson in perception, this exercise gives students a useful way to pass time in a theater when the movie starts dragging.

Granted the impossibility of taking in everything, writers can only give it their best shot. They need to push themselves to keep their senses switched on. Learning to get the most out of one's senses is not like learning the rules of capitalization, but the following writing workouts give direction to what should be a lifelong goal.

How to See When You Look:
Four Ways to Pay Attention

1. Look Around

Take an imaginary visitor on a tour of your daily route to work, school, or anywhere else you habitually travel. Put into words what you see. Describe the eccentric old man who every day leaves the rundown mansion at the corner of Morton and Main. Give details of the crumbling mansion. Keep adding to your tour as you learn the names of trees and churches along the route and notice for the first time the zigzag design on the facade of the Art Deco movie house.

Comment

Admittedly, this activity sounds rather like one of those suggestions enthusiastic teachers throw out with little expectation that anyone will actually take them up on it. Something like, "Next time you happen by the public library, why not drop in and sample the complete works of Immanuel Kant?" In a classroom, you'll need a way to bring such challenges down to earth.

Here's one way I get the less-than-motivated tuned in to daily observation. I give regular and brief reports on what I see on the way to work: "The ancient barber with the shop at 20th and Irving now opens his shop at 7:30 A.M. He sits, reading the same issue of *People* magazine, but no customers enter."

I ask for volunteers to report in a like manner. I tell the students that, within a couple of weeks, I will want them to write, in class, an account of tour highlights along their route. This announcement, as Dr. Johnson said in another context, "concentrates the mind wonderfully."

---

2. Eavesdrop

Enjoy the overheard details of other people's lives. Train yourself to remember them. Listen to the words of the couple at the restaurant sniping toward a divorce or the grandmothers on the subway exchanging tales of how their children never visit them. Stop on the stairs at a party. Listen. Recall and record this talk later, keeping the original language but editing for emphasis.

Comment

I encourage kids to eavesdrop because I see it as a healthy way to get them outside themselves, to counter the normal but sometimes compulsive tendency toward adolescent self-obsession. Although every lively person I know eavesdrops, my advocacy of this practice in my classroom has sometimes led adults to accuse me of corrupting the youth. If so, pass the hemlock; I am not going to stop now.

"Hear everything you can while you still have two good ears," I tell students.

This general advice, however, needs more direction. Over a week, I ask students to pull, from separate overheard conversations, three sentences or phrases worthy of a head turn. They exchange these conversation snatches and then use one of the received pieces of conversation in a dialogue, placing it neither at the beginning nor the end. The idea is not so much to practice dialogue writing as it is to encourage thinking about what one overhears. Here are few of many dozens of conversation snatches that have proved inspirational:

"But she has both the Cliffs and the Monarchs."

"It was one of those beds that has, like, a canopy."

"He scored humungous SATs. That's his problem."

3. Take a Breath

Put your nose and your mind to work at the same time. Make a list of animals, objects, and substances that produce odor. Here are some to get started:

- sea air
- wet wool
- disinfectant
- wood
- marijuana
- dogs
- cat boxes
- old milk
- hairspray
- fresh laundry

- soap
- grass
- incense
- skunks
- garbage
- garlic
- chili
- popcorn
- leather
- new books

- new cars
- whiskey
- candles
- pine needles
- coffee
- sewage
- tobacco smoke
- feet
- french fries

Now mix some smells together to suggest a location as Edvins Beitiks does in this catalogue of the smells of Greenwich Village on a hot summer evening:

> *... the perfume of women losing layers of soap to the heat, of cardboard pizza, of hand-carried trash, of dogs and strong coffee and a light salt wave from the Hudson River.*

4. Pretend You Are Taking Pictures

You can bring the world into focus, make your surroundings less of an amorphous blur, if you make mental snapshots. Remember, however, the best picture to take away may not be of the happy couple cutting the wedding cake, but rather of the pouty ex-boyfriend looking on from the corner.

When you take a trip or attend an event, set as a goal two or three mental photographs you can reconstruct later.

A first-time visitor to rural coastal Northern California brings back a mind picture:

> *... a decrepit Volkswagen bus covered with peace symbols, its greasy engine parts arranged on the ground, pondered by a thin shirtless man with a foot-long ponytail.*

And she also records another mental snapshot:

> *... a bulletin board outside a general store announcing in hand-printed letters a town meeting, a vegetarian potluck to benefit the school art program, a request for a ride to Mexico.*

The head pictures you bring back can be expanded with further observation and comment.

ENLIGHTENMENT FOR BEGINNERS:
THREE WAYS TO USE WHAT YOU SEE

Essay

Beyond Just Looking

THE world gives us the raw material; we provide the meaning. The girl comes to my desk after class. She starts blurting short sentences, blinking, her hands working the air. Her voice is up a pitch or two. Although she is telling a sad tale, she is wearing a fixed smile. The girl is lying.

Her story is about the essay she doesn't have. She was absent on the day it was assigned or she left it in the back of her mother's car or her niece used it for coloring paper.

While I know she is not telling the truth, I am not going to confront her. The circumstances are not worth a public scene. I'll accept her late work, attach a nominal penalty, and try not to take this fibbing personally. After all, I am thinking, if Mother Theresa assigned Term Projects, she, too, would be listening to these wild stories.

But why am I so sure she is lying? My experience helps me figure out what is going on. I am connecting the pieces of behavior I am witnessing to other tales, other due dates.

Part of our job as teachers of writing is to push students along the road to making more sophisticated meaning from their observation. Here are some ways to encourage students to go beyond just looking.

1. Reflect on What You See

A basic way to get thinking about your experience is to play the Who/What/How/Why Game. Keep a question journal in which you ask yourself about what you see. You can find or invent answers, but the answers aren't as important as the questions. Just asking gets you thinking.

How did the traffic crossing guard get the money for the Mercedes? Why is the usually grouchy bus driver so happy this morning? What has happened to the three homeless people who used to sleep in the doorways along the bus route?

Sometimes you'll hit on a question about which you have a lot to say. In that case keep writing.

Comment

Nobody will find me criticizing any teacher's journal projects. The claims for journal keeping are mostly true, if, perhaps, too often repeated. Journal keeping leads writers to discover themselves, to learn better particular subjects, and to investigate the world in general. Journal keeping, however, does demand dedication and discipline, which are in fact two of its strengths as a teaching tool.

By contrast, the question journal which I propose here, while not replacing more rigorous forms of journal making, requires but minutes a day, particularly if the questions are only recorded and mulled over. Some "answers" can come later. I expect students to ask themselves four questions a day. Once a week, I ask them for their two favorite questions for that week. After a few weeks of persistent question asking, habits form. I like to think that long after students stop recording questions they will still be asking them.

Here are a few questions from my students that range from mundane to profound. They were all inspired by observation:

- *Who is checking to determine if store owners are selling cigarettes to minors? What happens if an owner is caught?*

- *Why doesn't my father watch Monday Night Football like all the other dads I know? What makes some people interested in some things and other people interested in other things?*
- *How does an automatic teller machine work?*
- *Why does a kiss feel good?*
- *Who makes up the SAT questions? How do they know your score will show how you will perform in college?*

2. Connect Your Observations

Play the Hookup Game. A few years ago, a writer noticed open kitchens in restaurants, a panel of sex addicts on the Donahue show, wristwatches with see-through faces, Demi Moore posing bare and pregnant on the cover of *Vanity Fair*.

She made a hookup: all of the above are evidence of the modern itch to expose what was once considered private. She was generalizing from a series of observations; that's inductive reasoning.

Or a writer may work the other way around, starting with the idea and then collecting the evidence to support it; that's deductive reasoning. For instance, the only reason you know a recession is going on is because they keep telling you so on the Evening News. But then you start to look around. You notice more people are in the park on a weekday feeding the ducks, and, for the first time, at eleven o'clock Saturday morning, there is no problem getting a parking place at the shopping mall. You have seen the recession.

Focus on one of the following statements which you can accept as generally true. Note every observation which confirms this belief. Although you will not want to exclude what you read and what you are told by others, you should rely as much as possible on what you have seen.

- *Religion is on the rise (or it isn't).*
- *The Era of Greed has ended (or it hasn't).*
- *Safe sex and abstinence have caught on (or they haven't).*
- *Americans are fed up with traditional politics or (they aren't).*
- *Environmental concerns get more attention today (or they don't).*
- *There is growing harmony between the races (or there isn't).*
- *Crime is a major concern in the United States (or it isn't).*

Comment

With at least some students, you'll be better off with generalizations closer to home.

- *School spirit is on the rise (or it isn't).*
- *At school, we are treated equally, regardless of race, religion, and gender (or we aren't).*

Students can brainstorm observations in small groups or as a class.

I have been using deduction workouts for many years, sometimes with surprising results. Back in the early eighties, I presented students with the findings of the sociologist Erving Goffman, who had studied gender roles in advertising. Goffman concluded that when a man and woman appeared in a magazine ad photo, the man almost always appeared to be in charge, placed above the woman. The woman was likely to be leaning on the man. I asked students to examine ad photos to see if their findings supported Goffman's generalization. A little exercise in deduction. The support was almost always there. Dusting off this activity in the early nineties, and expecting the same results, I was surprised when students concluded exactly the opposite. Now women were on top and in charge. Some even carried pool cues.

Advertising mirrors cultural values. Put your students to work on this. Have some make generalizations after collecting evidence, and others find evidence in support of generalizations.

3. Allow Your Experience to Inform Your Observation

Say it's the fourth quarter when you turn on the TV broadcast of the football game. You don't know the score, but the cameraman treats you to a close-up of one of your team's players sitting alone on the bench, a blanket pulled over his head. You know the news is not good.

The longer you live, the more you understand.

For instance, consider the lives of the people who stock their refrigerators with the different contents below. What do you know about them and why?

Number One: Three kinds of champagne, three kinds of imported beer, three kinds of mineral water, three kinds of eggs, two kinds of paté, four kinds of cheeses, four kinds of mustard, two magnums of white wine.

Number Two: Jello salad, three half-gallons of milk, giant sizes of mustard and catsup, a pitcher of Kool-Aid, peanut butter, six kinds of yogurt, a loaf of Wonder Bread, four cans of American beer, large jars of spaghetti sauce, a triple batch of marinated chicken, several casseroles.

Number Three: Thirteen cans of beer, slices of supermarket salami, a foul smelling quart of milk, leftovers of a frozen macaroni and cheese dinner, a piece of Swiss cheese turned hard around the edges.

You can put your experience to work on some similar observations. You may not have access to many refrigerators, but the contents of supermarket shopping carts are worth studying.

Comment

You can make this challenge for students a bit more formal. For homework, send them to a supermarket to list shopping cart contents. In class, figure out what some of these lists tell you.

BRINGING OUT THE INNER EYE:
FOUR WAYS TO WRITE FROM MEMORY

Essay

ON rainy weekend days when I was a kid of about ten we would look around our drawers, basements, and closets and come up with a pile of knick-knacks and junk. We would then take turns arranging on a tray about twenty of these items—the Hoover for President button, the paper weight from the 1939 San Francisco Exposition, the Captain Midnight Decoder. We'd study the tray for about three minutes, take it away, and see which of us could remember the most items. This was fun for a while, but the same kid—Roger was his name—always won. Not only would he rattle off all the items on the day we played, but if you asked two weeks later he would tell you again. Roger moved away, but years later when I started thinking about what writers do, I realized, that with his memory, Roger would have been one up on many in the craft if he had decided to be a writer. I heard later Roger made a lot of money in real estate. I doubt he ever forgot a floor plan.

The following writing workouts are not guaranteed to turn students into tray game champions, but they will remind them of the connection between remembering and writing.

1. Re-see Objects

Practice summoning phantom versions of familiar shapes. For instance, you've seen pictures of the Academy Award statuette, Oscar, dozens of times. Now, before you read on, describe it in as much detail as possible.

If you said Oscar is gold-plated, sleek, without clearly defined features, apparently male, bald, rigidly standing on a base, and holding chest-high the handle of a sword, the tip of which rests at his feet, your mind's eye is right in focus.

With practice, you can get better at re-creation. Here are some objects you've seen many times. Turn on your mental movie projector and remember as much as possible about their appearance.

- *a monopoly board*
- *a postal carrier's uniform*
- *your state flag*
- *the Statue of Liberty*
- *a Campbell's Soup can*
- *the Frankenstein monster*
- *a one dollar bill*
- *the cover of National Geographic*

Try these re-creations in a group of people. Challenge each other with other distinctive objects.

2. Trust Your Memory

Recall and narrate a first meeting or a last farewell with a special person. Re-create the event in as much detail as possible: the personalities, the setting, the dialogue, the action.

These details may not come all at once. However, do not be deterred. Imagine what you do not specifically recall. You will probably be right in the feeling, if not the particulars. If, for instance, you remember how at age six you and your friend Peggy devoured chocolate ice cream cones together minutes before she left forever for Alaska, and you remember spilling a good part of the ice cream on your dress, but you do not remember the color of the dress, make the dress any color that seems right. If you get it wrong, who's going to know?

3. Document Change

Remember how things used to be. This may seem like a habit of the older generation who recall a world before bar codes, VCRs, and MTV. Your parents or other relatives may remember, for example, entering airports where they could walk freely to their flights without being subjected to metal detectors, then entering a plane where they would be greeted by stewardesses, not cabin attendants representing both genders.

You may not remember those days, but if you are over twelve, you too live in a vastly different world than you did a few years ago.

Remember and write about specific changes that have occurred in your lifetime in some of the following or other areas, concentrating on what you have seen, not only what you have read about.

- *Saturday cartoons*
- *scary movies*
- *haircuts*
- *radio station formats*
- *telephones*
- *toys*
- *a professional sport*
- *popular music*
- *attitudes toward dating, sex, marriage*
- *computers*

4. Connect Past Feelings to Present Circumstances

You'll notice that while the situations of your life change, the same feelings—anxiety, say, or infatuation—keep coming up. As a writer, you can make use of these recurring emotions by connecting a present feeling to its past incarnations.

Here a writer explains his feelings while watching a presidential debate by referring to other times he has had the same feelings.

> *The last debate is tonight. How to explain the existential terror of knowing that in less than a month you'll have to choose one of these guys as president. Who can watch them? It's like listening to your parents argue, complete with the horrible smiles and assurances of mutual respect. You just want it to stop.*
>
> *It's like being stuck in a car pool with somebody who insists on explaining the difference between whole and term life insurance to you, morning after morning, and you know it's important, and there are differences, but you just want it to stop.*
> —Henry Allen, *Washington Post*

Consider a recent event that inspired a strong feeling. Relate this event and feeling to past times when you have had a similar feeling.

Some possibilities:

- euphoria
- generosity
- solemnity
- respect
- contempt
- selfishness
- impatience
- awe
- humility
- nervousness
- forgiveness
- pity

Part III: Writers Think First

- **Clearing Cobwebs, Breaking Molds:**
  Five Probes to Fresh Thinking

- **Making Sense:**
  Thirteen Ways to Sharpen Your Opinion

On Making Waves

I T'S the morning of November 22, 1963, and I am asking my eighth grade social studies students, "What happens if the President dies in office?" By that afternoon we will begin to find out, and only some of the answers will be detailed in Article II, Section 6, of the United States Constitution.

The assassinations, scams, and cover-ups which followed in the decades after JFK's death are supposed to have made cynics of us all. All, that is, except lots of kids age fifteen and a half who continue to believe the best of people. I have observed that beyond their sometimes sullen MTV exteriors and their often intimate knowledge of adult nastiness, most kids work hard at being idealists. Ignoring evidence to the contrary, they would still rather believe Anne Frank than Bart Simpson. In prodding students to think, a teacher needs to take some middle ground between being a Pollyanna and a spoilsport.

Looking back, I will admit to having been the gadfly, sometimes too eager to stir things up.

I once enjoyed confronting students, for example, with the research of the sociologist Frederick Meeker who contended romantic love has a chance of remaining steamy for no more than ninety days, and that to believe anything else is to fool oneself into accepting a total "farce." I asked students to use their experience to argue for or against Meeker. Of course, many students who had watched their parents split up and felt their own adolescent ardors cool, sided with Meeker. What I remember, however, is Melissa Barrett's poignant resistance to the sociologist's jaded worldliness. "Just because it is a total farce," she wrote, "doesn't mean we shouldn't believe in it."

After a while, I came to see that my real work was not so much to puncture students' beliefs as to encourage them to examine their own doubts.

CLEARING COBWEBS, BREAKING MOLDS:
FIVE PROBES TO FRESH THINKING

1. Dig into Your Beliefs

Think about the connection between your bedrock beliefs and the way you live. If, for instance, you believe that nature has created all animals for the benefit of man, you'll probably find nothing unethical about eating cow for dinner. You are not likely to demonstrate in front of the supermarket carrying a "Meat is Murder" placard. Start with the assumption that all work is ennobling and you'll be more likely to rally some enthusiasm for scrubbing the gunk out of the grout in the shower stall.

Here are some values statements about important matters. Find some with which you agree or disagree. Write about how these beliefs translate into specific action *for you*. Give examples. For instance, if you value friendship more than personal integrity, you'll be more likely to let a friend copy your exam answers.

- *Loyalty to one's friends is more important than loyalty to one's family.*
- *Security is more important than wealth.*
- *Creative work is more important than socially useful work.*
- *Friendship is more important than personal integrity.*
- *Duty to one's family is more important than personal success.*
- *Physical and emotional safety are more important than sensual pleasure.*
- *Personal integrity is more important than financial success.*

Probe other conflicting values. Write about how these values decisions affect your behavior.

2. Examine Your Confusions

You can think about a question that confuses you by stepping back from it. Become, for the moment, both yourself and an inquiring space alien. The alien asks the hard questions; you try to answer.

Here's what the beginning of a self-interview with an alien might look like. The alien is wondering why women wear high heels:

Alien: *Why do women put these things on their feet?*
Answer: *Many say heels make their legs look longer, their bodies "sexy."*
Question: *Where do they get such beliefs?*
Answer: *From men. Men set standards of beauty and sex appeal in a male-dominated culture.*
Question: *But don't some women enjoy heels for their own sake?*
Answer: *Are you kidding? Does anybody think women would wear heels in an all-female society? Women think high heels are sexy because men are turned on by high heels…*
—Charles Burress

Invite the Creature from Another Planet to interview you as you explain your views on one of the following or a similar issue:

Why do some people live in great luxury in your nation while others have nothing?

Why is marijuana illegal in your country while tobacco is not?

Why do people of different colors live in different neighborhoods?

Why do teachers and nurses make smaller salaries than baseball players and rock performers?

Why are prostitutes arrested?

Why are there so many different brands of cereal in the supermarket?

3. Choose Among Values

In the following news account of a restaurant incident, the food servers, customer, and restaurant manager all make values choices. What are the choices? What would you do if you were each of these people?

> *A waiter and waitress fired from a gourmet hamburger restaurant in Seattle for balking at serving alcohol to a pregnant woman vow to take their case to court.*
>
> *The waiter, G. R. Heryford, said he was concerned about the health risk to the customer's unborn child and asked her whether she knew about the dangers of drinking alcohol while pregnant. He said the woman, who had ordered a strawberry daiquiri, replied, "The baby's past due—it had its chance."*
>
> *Heryford said he told his co-workers about the situation, and a waitress, Danita Fitch, decided to show the woman the surgeon general's warning about pregnant women drinking alcohol.*
>
> *Heryford said, "The lady immediately got very upset, jumped up, ran to the hostess' desk, and demanded to see the manager. The lady proceeded to ream him out."*
>
> *Both Heryford and Fitch were called into the manager's office ten minutes later and summarily fired.*
>
> *A spokesman for the restaurant said the restaurant's primary business is to "provide quality service to customers, not to belittle them in front of other patrons."*

Draw on your experience to tell a story of values in conflict. Try writing it in the form of a news report as in the above account.

In Praise of Triviality

MAKING a presentation before a group of teachers who don't want to be there can be scary. Performing in a captive situation before a classroom of teenagers, I have at my service grades, diplomas, detentions, suspensions, and other carrots and sticks which combine to nudge many adolescents toward an unnatural tolerance for authority. By contrast, adults at a "mandatory" workshop who drift off to read the sports page or record pop quiz grades cannot be sent to the dean. And the ones who *do* pay attention can really stir things up. I remember one woman who asked, "How can you have students writing about their experiences with wrong number telephone calls when they live in a world of drugs, guns, violence, pregnancy, and AIDS?"

And then *I* said—I would not be telling this story if I did not have a pretty good answer—"Because if it is true that these things are part of students' lives, they are probably thinking about these important and depressing subjects all the time. Of course, they should write about them, but they also probably have had some experience with wrong numbers and may never have thought much about their reaction. Part of my job is to jolt students into taking a fresh look at their experience." Sometimes unexamined, even trivial topics that do not come bundled in a security blanket of clichés are the best vehicles to encourage fresh thinking.

4. Get Mad

Look around for some little things that bother you. Not the large, dark concerns that anger, or should anger, everyone—war, hunger, tyranny, for instance. This time look for something small that has made the world a worse place. Unleash your verbal wrath. You will almost surely write well and, with the adrenaline flowing, perhaps generate some new ideas and creative solutions.

For inspiration, look over these answers to a student journalist's question, "What really irritates you?" Of course, some or all of the items on this list of other students' annoyances may cause you no problem at all.

- *spirit rallies*
- *voice mail and answering machines*
- *people who break into supermarket express lanes when they have more than ten items*
- *proms*
- *golden oldies radio*
- *athletes who charge for autographs*
- *New Year's Eve parties*
- *people who never say "hello" back*
- *Sunday morning church bells*
- *double dates for proms*
- *TV news about fires and auto accidents*
- *complicated grading systems*
- *books by ex-celebrities that are mostly about who they've slept with*
- *"My child is an honor student at XXX School" bumper strips*
- *group work*
- *school ring promotions*
- *requirement to "take notes for a possible quiz" when students give boring oral reports*

Example: The following example was inspired by an item on one woman's list of irritations. She is a businesswoman at a writing workshop letting loose her pent-up anger toward those who hold cellular phone conversations in restaurants:

> *I belong to the old school. Some activities should be kept private: teeth flossing, French kissing, phone talk. With the invention of the cellular phone, the public display of the last of these is getting out of hand. Now, any Century Twenty One real estate salesman can play at being Donald Trump by plunking his portable phone down on the restaurant table and dialing frenetically, ignoring the sand dabs. OK, the business of America has always been business and this obsession has been no less widespread between the hours of 12 noon and 1:30 P.M. But the old three-martini lunch added up to two people, a little liar's dice, some jokes, and maybe a deal. Nothing to destroy what is supposed to be the restaurant's purpose as a place to relax, talk, and eat.*
>
> *Now that's changed. There are always at least two Type A candidates for the intensive care unit wheeling and dealing over the phone, stabbing the air with the hand unencumbered by the receiver. I am not spending $12.50 for a Shrimp Louie in order to eat in an atmosphere increasingly reminiscent of peak trading hours at the Chicago Commodities Exchange. Of course, it may sometimes be necessary to interrupt one's lunch for a telephone call. But that's why God invented the phone booth, like the bedroom and the bathroom, an ideal venue for activities best conducted in private.*

Should Creativity Be Compulsory?

EACH semester it is the same thing. "This is your chance to be creative," I practically whoop, but students do not begin dancing in the aisles. For a teenager, required cleverness is just one more requirement, imposed at a time when a lot of growing up is learning routines. Moreover, they, like the rest of us, find comfort in platitudes. On the day of the first rain of the year, for example, we are encouraged by tradition to dust off old saws: We make tired jokes about how this is good weather for ducks and comment on how much the farmers need the rain. No one gets points for originality here.

Given this toleration of, even preference for, the banal, it is not easy to explain to a student why her essay titled "Education: Key to the Future" with its ordered paragraphs, well-oiled transitions, and faultless spelling deserves a "C." Sure, every idea, value and word is predictable, but if predictability were universally recognized as a bad thing, "Three's Company" would never have thrived in cable reruns.

About the best I can do to inspire creativity is to spotlight escapes from the prosaic as they come along in student writing: the paper boy who details the special joys of being up at 4:30 A.M.; the student, now back in class after an almost fatal accident, who argues that all hospital workers—doctors to orderlies—should be paid the same; the seemingly gregarious girl who finds the best moments of her birthday party to be the half hour after everyone leaves. In front of the class, I'll call attention to these made-from-scratch ideas because, while creativity cannot be taught, it can be copied.

5. Spotlight the Unexpected

Find a "double take" idea, a statement that will startle a reader or listener into asking, "How's that again?" Most of us can agree that the words, "You get out of life what you put into it," provide a useful slogan to live by, but why not move on to a proposition that may be less often repeated, perhaps less true, but also more provocative? Look for ideas that take issue with the conventional wisdom, or call attention to what many are thinking but few are saying, or challenge widely held beliefs or respected institutions. One catch though: In order to be convincing, you need to believe what you are saying.

Below is a hodgepodge of ideas likely to draw responses ranging from, "Gee, I wish I'd said that," to "Are you crazy?"

Add to the list. Then pick a statement or two and develop the arguments.

- *The Post Office does a pretty good job.*
- *Orchestras would play just as well if no one were conducting.*
- *Every production of Shakespeare should be drastically cut to make it relevant to modern audiences.*
- *People who eat junk food suffer from self-loathing.*
- *Usually, we fall in love when we are bored with ourselves and with our lives. Falling in love and announcing your condition to the world is mostly a method of making yourself seem important.*
- *"Fun for the Whole Family" is impossible.*
- *A lot of people don't care if life goes on or not. That's why it's hard to get anyone excited about saving the environment.*
- *Beauty contests have nothing to do with men taking pleasure in ogling half-clothed women. Give a man a choice between a Miss this or that pageant and a Mets game, he'll go for the game every time. Beauty contests are for women.*
- *Let's not wring our hands about voter "apathy" among the eighteen- to twenty-one-year olds. When they don't vote, they are sim-*

ply acting their age. They have other things on their mind and should never have been given the vote in the first place.

- *Children are cruel, ruthless, cunning, and incredibly self-centered. Far from cementing a marriage, children more frequently disrupt it. Child rearing is on the whole an expensive and unrewarding bore, in which more has to be invested both materially and spiritually than ever comes out in dividends.* (Nigel Ballchin, 1965)
- *If a writer has to rob his mother, he will not hesitate; the "Ode to a Grecian Urn" is worth any number of old ladies.* (William Faulkner)

Comment

Lively ideas aren't hard to come by. You can help students by brainstorming with them expressions of conventional wisdom that just about everyone is supposed to believe: The food in the school cafeteria is terrible. ... Among teenagers, the strongest friendships exist between members of the same sex.

Most students will be able to find one of these "Everybody knows" ideas about which they have serious, perhaps secret, doubts. They should find it liberating to explain their beliefs.

Making Sense:
Thirteen Ways to Sharpen Your Opinions

Essay

The Struggle to Be Reasonable

MANY of the challenges in this chapter touch on principles of logic, an area of study that, frankly, makes me squirm. It's not that I don't know my stuff. I can spot someone else's genetic fallacy or post hoc ergo hoc argument before it leaves the starting gate. It's just that, in the privacy of my own home, I am no stranger myself to false analogies, hasty generalizations, and off-the-wall non sequiturs. Watching the evening news, I sometimes hear myself saying things like, "If he weren't guilty, he wouldn't pull his coat over his head."

Standing in front of a class, then, speaking of terms like "ambiguity" and "equivocation" leaves me feeling vaguely hypocritical. I am behaving too much like the con man played by Sydney Greenstreet in "The Maltese Falcon," cynically toasting "plain speech and clear understanding."

However, if all persons who sometimes succumb to irrational mental detours were prohibited from teaching logic, logic teachers would be in short supply. It may be my unreasonable private opinion that anyone who dyes his hair orange or takes Michael Bolton seriously lacks the character and judgment to be President. Yet in my role as a teacher I can still stand foursquare against the argument ad hominem.

The larger point here is that sweet reason is a rare commodity among both students and teachers. A certain humility is in order. We are all in this together.

1. Define Key Words

If your argument depends on a shared understanding of "truth" and "justice," you need to explain to your reader exactly what you mean by these words.

The hipster art critic can claim that "there is more real art in the graffiti scrawled on the sides of city buses than in all of this town's galleries and museums put together." But what does he mean by "art?"

A slippery writer may try to make an emotional point by using an undefined word in a quirky and customized way. Here's an experiment to give you some practice with this customized use of language.

1. Give your off-the-top-of-the-head definition of each word below.
2. Check your definition against a dictionary definition.
3. Decide if either or both of these definitions are consistent with the way the word is used in each of the statements that follow.

The Words

- genocide
- litter
- communism
- obscenity
- freedom
- democracy
- violence
- murder

- A person who, while driving drunk, kills someone in a traffic accident is as much a *murderer* as someone who unloads an Uzi in a shopping mall.
- It is unfair to condemn *communism* as a social and economic system because real *communism* hasn't been tried.
- The U. S. Constitution guarantees our *freedom*, yet we arrest nude sunbathers exercising their *freedom* on a public beach.
- Scientific experiments on helpless animals are no less a form of *genocide* than the Nazi medical experiments on the Jews.

- The growing gap between rich and poor is the most glaring *obscenity* of our time.
- How can we claim the United States is a *democracy* when less than half the nation's eligible voters turn out at election time?
- It's not the beer can tossed from the pickup truck that creates *litter*, it's the road itself which is the *litter*.
- We oppose all types of *violence* on children's television, from superhero mayhem to Bugs Bunny pouring a pitcher of milk over the head of a chipmunk.

Comment

Students should be encouraged to consider the customized application of these highly charged words as neither "right" nor "wrong." The workout is intended to prod students into a discussion of the slippery nature of language.

---

2. Question Vagueness

Cross-examine your language. Pull the fuzzy terms from your opinions and ask yourself what you really mean by them.

OK, if "desecration of the American flag should be against the law," just what does "desecration" mean? Is it "desecration" to:

- make a flag in shades of green as an ecological symbol?
- make a flag in putrid green, a symbol of a sick nation?
- sew a fifty-first star on the flag and put Elizabeth Taylor's picture in the center of the star?
- burn a flag?
- burn an old flag?
- burn the flag to which you have added the fifty-first star?
- burn a black and white photograph of the flag?
- burn a color photograph of the flag?
- burn a paper flag lapel pin?
- try unsuccessfully to burn a flag made out of flame-resistant material?

Ask probing questions about the slippery words in one of the following opinions or in a similar one:

- People become more "conservative" as they grow older.
- First-born children get more "advantages" than others in the family.
- An "unfaithful" couple can still have a "good marriage."
- "Creative" people are usually a "little crazy."
- The "cultural elite" does not respect "family values."

3. Distinguish Facts from Opinions

Use facts when you have them. What you know is at least as important as what you think.

In logic, a fact is a piece of information which is accurate or can be shown to be inaccurate. Using this definition, a false statement like "The moon is made of Ben and Jerry's crunchy monkey ice cream" is a "fact" because its reliability can be disproved. You need to be able to recognize a fact when you see one. Here are ten statements about pregnancy and abortion. Five of them are facts. Which five?

1. It is immoral to arrest anti-abortion protesters who believe they are exercising their right of free speech by blocking access to abortion clinics.
2. Pro-choice policies will be in jeopardy so long as men control the political system.
3. The number of abortions performed in the United States has remained about level since 1979.
4. An abortion is ten times less likely to cause medical problems than carrying a pregnancy to term.
5. Most of the officers in the national pro-choice organizations are white women with above-average incomes.
6. If the unborn could be heard, they would be one-hundred percent pro-life.
7. Women have an innate need to give birth.
8. Forty percent of fourteen-year-old girls will become pregnant before they are out of their teens.
9. The Supreme Court has said, "The right of privacy ... is broad enough to encompass a woman's decision whether or not to terminate her pregnancy."
10. The right to privacy implied by the Constitution should be enough to protect a woman's right to terminate her pregnancy.

Answers: Facts—3, 4, 5, 8, 9

Now:

1. Find a photograph that interests you.

2. Make a list of facts you draw from your observation of the photograph.
   Example: A boy and girl pose for a prom photo. She wears what looks like a boy's class ring around her neck. They are not touching each other.

3. Make a list of opinions suggested by the photograph.
   Example: They are a steady couple. They may soon be available to date others.
   Example: She's going steady with someone else and in a fit of anger agreed to go to the prom with this boy. She now regrets her decision.

4. Integrate into a coherent paragraph some of these facts and opinions.

Nitpicking: The Curse of the Pedant Class

I am, half-mindlessly, commenting on student papers.

Student draft one reads: "Cigarettes should not be banned. The government cannot ban everything that is dangerous for people. Chocolate is bad for people, but no one says we should ban it."

I scribble, "What's so dangerous about chocolate?"

Draft two reads: "Cigarettes should not be banned. The government cannot ban everything that is bad for people. Chocolate, which causes acne, is bad for people, but no one says we should ban it."

Fortunately or not, I have heard that chocolate does *not* cause acne. What to do?

1. Forget the whole thing, The kid did try to supply some evidence. Does it matter that it is incorrect?

2. Correct the error. As a teacher I must be committed to upholding truth and rectifying error.

3. Treat the fact as if it is true in order to ask a question about a more serious lapse in logic: "Is acne equivalent to the lung cancer and heart disease caused by cigarettes?"

I opt for number 3. Sometimes, to correct a fact is to pick a nit. Often, to question logic is to clear a head.

Essay

Sources

WHEN I was sixteen, a friend gave me an interesting fact: Every time you eat a slice of pizza, the Mafia gets four cents. I think it was the four cents that sold me. People, I reasoned, don't make up that kind of precision.

A couple of years later, my freshman English teacher asked us to write a short paper "taking a strong stand on some event in the news." As it happened, this was the very week that beefy mobsters were pleading the Fifth Amendment before the Senate Rackets Committee. I had found my topic. I wrote, "The activities of the mob go beyond the activities being described at the hearings. They affect our daily lives. Every time you eat a slice of pizza, the Mafia gets six cents." I was adjusting for inflation.

Our papers were returned—with comment. Secretly, my teacher may have been distressed that such an unlikely candidate for a college degree as I had evaded the admission officer's watchful eye. However, on my paper, all she asked about my pizza allegation was, "How do you know this?"

This got me thinking about the guy who had told me about the pizza connection. He was also the one who once insisted that tennis balls were filled with poison gas, a fact I now knew to be false.

In the years that I have been teaching, when confronted by unsubstantiated claims in student writing, like the insistence that the Pentagon keeps a file of who scores the highest on video games, or, more recently, the allegation that the Ku Klux Klan owns Church's Chicken and puts something in it to make African American men sterile, my first question is always the same as my old instructor's: "How do you know this?"

4. Distinguish Between Opinions Which Can Be Supported with Evidence and Those Which Can't Be

You've heard the standard advice for making an argument: support you opinions with facts. A sound suggestion, except for those of your opinions which are unprovable hunches or judgments of values or taste. In these cases, facts aren't all that useful.

If you believed that the fifty-five-mile-an-hour speed limit was dangerous and uneconomical, you could find many facts in the library to support this view—as well as its opposite. However, if you want to convince us that our purpose in life is to help others, the library's fact collection will be of little use, except as a source of quotes from other people who agree with you.

Look at each of the statements below. Can the opinion be supported by facts? (You aren't expected to know the facts that could be used as support.) In several cases, the opinion is so loose and vague that the discreet course would be to abandon the whole idea. Other opinions can be modified to make them more defensible.

1. A firm handshake is a sign of good character.
2. In general, people who were of college age in the 1960s have less respect for authority than people of earlier generations.
3. The Superbowl is a ritual to reaffirm our values as a nation. It's all we represent as a country being crystallized in pursuit of success, fighting for a higher value: the team.
4. The United States is a neurotic country.
5. The people of the United States are more health conscious than the people of most Western European countries.
6. The United States is an economically wealthy country compared to other countries in the world.
7. Lots of curved-legged furniture in a house indicates the occupant has a passive, yielding nature.
8. The will of the majority is the great foe of freedom.

9. A translation of a great work of literature can never match the beauty of the original.
10. The reason Americans love to watch violence on television is because so many of them lead tedious, uneventful lives.
11. Unlike the movie stars of a previous era, very few of the current crop of Hollywood celebrities know which fork to use at a dinner party.

Note the next five opinions you hear or read. Which could be supported or disputed with facts?

Comment

The comments which follow are intended to push students to distinguish between views that are mostly rhetorical smoke and those which can be defended with factual evidence or other arguments.

1. *A firm handshake is a sign of good character.* Hard to defend. What is good character? Beyond that, the writer must depend on her own experience with handshakes or, perhaps, what she has read about the steely grip of some highly moral person.
2. *In general, people who were of college age in the 1960s have less respect for authority than people of earlier generations.* One could call on anecdotal evidence from the sixties and recent polls and interviews with people who were in college then.
3. *The Superbowl is a ritual to reaffirm…* Empty rhetoric which can be supported only by more empty rhetoric.
4. *The United States is a neurotic country.* How can a nation be neurotic? We are in the realm of metaphor, not fact.
5. and 6. *The people of the United States are more health conscious than the people of most Western European countries. The United States is an economically wealthy country*

... Both these claims could be supported or countered with statistics.

7. *Lots of curved-legged furniture indicates the occupant has a passive, yielding nature.* Fanciful and unprovable claim, but just the kind of assertion that some anecdotal evidence could turn into an amusing essay.

8. *The will of the majority is the great foe of freedom.* One of those generalizations that is so large that there is plenty of historical evidence on both sides. But first, what is "freedom?"

9. *A translation of a great work of literature can never match the beauty of the original.* No way to prove this statement, which is about taste. Also, the "never" expands the statement to include all translations, past and future. No way.

10. *The reason Americans love to watch violence on television is because so many of them lead tedious, uneventful lives.* This opinion sets up a vague and unprovable cause-effect relationship. Contrast this claim, for instance, with the statement, "Television violence leads to real-life violence," an opinion solid enough to be researched.

11. *Unlike the movie stars of a previous era, very few of the current crop of Hollywood celebrities know which fork to use at a dinner party.* An idea that could be defended with a selective use of evidence—David Niven on the one hand, Mickey Rourke on the other.

Essay

The Ashley Syndrome:
Breakdowns on the Route from Narrative to Exposition

ASHLEY, age sixteen, writes an observation of her eighteen-year-old brother on a morning after he has been partying: *He slumps at the kitchen table, picking at his corn flakes, wearing only Jockey shorts. His face is a sickening yellow color, except for the red splotches that look like radioactive islands on a polluted sea. He pushes aside his World's Greatest Lover coffee mug, shakes a Marlboro from the pack, drops the cigarette, picks it up, and puts the wrong end in his mouth.*

Ashley presents a vivid portrait of a likely candidate for a Just Say No Poster Boy.

A few months later, Ashley, age sixteen-and-a-half, writes an analysis of George Orwell's essay, "Shooting an Elephant": *Imperialism is symbolized by the actions of Orwell in this story. But at the same time, fear among everyone is also mixed with excitement.*

How's that again?

Ashley, like thousands before her, has abandoned a powerful narrative and descriptive style and plunged into a mishmash of garbled expository and analytic prose.

I am not sure why this unfortunate transformation occurs, but I do know some ways to begin to counter it. For starters, as demonstrated in the following workout, one can practice anchoring general statements in facts and observations. The Ashley Syndrome is treatable and often not fatal.

5. Reinforce What You Think with What You Know

When an idea springs from what you read or see, don't stop there. Instead, confirm this insight by recalling other facts and observations which support this opinion. Here's how this meshing of information and ideas can work:

You *read* that in the original game of basketball there was a jump ball after every basket.

You *think* rules in sports are regularly changed to make the game more interesting.

You *remember* that once every basket counted for two points. Three-pointers were added to make the game more exciting.

You *read:* One hundred years ago a tourist shop at Niagara Falls sold little pieces of gypsum labeled, "Petrified Mist from the Falls."

You *think:* Lots of tourists are suckers.

You *remember:* A farmer in your state has made a lot of money selling admissions to a spot on his land where he claims a UFO has landed.

Consider the following facts. What idea does each generate? What have you seen or read which bolsters this generalization? You can do this as a game with one player providing the generalization, another the supporting evidence. Avoid generalizations which are clichés ("Everything happens for the best."), and discuss whether the new evidence really *does* support the generalization.

- Whistler painted his mother when his intended model didn't show up.
- Edward Rice Burroughs, creator of Tarzan, had never been to Africa.
- General U. S. Grant, head of the Union forces in the Civil War, was repelled by the sight of blood. Even rare red meat made him queasy.

- In 1966, the ratio of male to female ulcer patients was twenty to one. Now it is two to one.
- Police get usable fingerprints at only three out of one hundred crime scenes.
- The tradition of three meals a day is a convenience. Many nutritionists believe we would be healthier if we ate six small meals a day.
- Aristotle believed that one could judge a man's character by the shape of his nose.
- In the United States, there are twenty thousand astrologers but only two thousand astronomers.
- Despite the prominence of umbrellas in London, London does not get as many rainy days as New York City, Paris, or Tokyo.
- The French call syphilis the "English disease" and vice versa.
- A city dog lives on average eleven years, a country dog only eight.
- On the old "I Love Lucy" show, Ricky Ricardo was recognized as a Cuban until the Communist revolution in Cuba. He was then transformed into a Mexican.

Comment

No writing skill is more important than the ability to move confidently from specific statements to general ideas, and this workout reinforces the concept that general statements need to be moored in information and observation.

The process suggested here is easier than it looks. Here's how it works in my class. Each day I present a fact and we see where it leads us. Take, for instance, "Whistler painted his mother when his intended model didn't show up."

I show the class a print of the painting. (I have learned the hard way Rule 1 of classroom allusions: Never assume anyone knows anything.) The dialogue goes:

Maggie: *That his model didn't show up, is that what they call a "happy accident?"*

Me: *So how about a generalization?*

Saul: *Sometimes an inconvenience turns into something good.*

Abbey: *It's like the bad news turns into good news.*

Me: *How about, today's inconvenience may be tomorrow's good news.*

Saul: *My uncle had a dead battery just before he was getting ready to go across the Bay Bridge. That was the day part of the bridge collapsed in the earthquake. That fits.*

Jai: *How about the guy who let the food get moldy and accidentally discovered penicillin.*

Me: *Does that fit?*

And so on …

Five minutes a day of this for two months will do more for orderly thinking than a whole semester of diagramming syllogisms.

6. Be Fair

If your opinion is provocative, it probably isn't boring, but it may be unfair. Try out words that suggest the other side: "but," "also," "yet," "however," and "even though."

Example: Instead of *Shakespeare was a white male writer whose idea of a hero was a Scottish serial killer who heard voices.*

Try, *Yes, Shakespeare's characters include strong women, reasonable characters, and martyrs to good causes,* **yet** *Shakespeare could* **also** *raise to heroic status a Scottish serial killer who heard voices.*

Cool down and you may change minds rather than merely raise hackles. Try supplying details that give balance to the following strong opinions:

- Anyone who doubts that Americans can be apathetic about their democratic rights needs only be reminded that it wasn't long ago that a dog was elected mayor of Sunol, California. Yet… (contrasting specifics).
- There is an ugly side to man's curious nature. We are curious enough to gawk at the carnage of terrible car wrecks, curious enough to stop everything to watch two dogs rutting, curious enough to stay tuned while Geraldo probes civilization's underbelly. This needs to be said even though our curiosity has also led us to … (supply balancing specifics).
- To some, the cat is the ideal domestic pet only for those who wish to live with smells and snarls and scratches, with shredded rugs, and with a creature who is sneaky, selfish, disloyal, and dumb. But others don't share this negative caricature. To them a cat is … (contrasting specifics).

Team up with another person. On your own, write a one-sided and specific argument about some aspect of the American character (see "apathy" above), or human nature (see "curiosity") or a common possession (see "cats") Finish with a "but," "also," "yet," or "even though," and allow your partner to provide the rebuttal details.

7. Know When and How to Qualify Your Opinions

Make positive, sure-footed statements whenever you can:

> *The age of chivalry is gone. That of the sophists, economists, and calculators has succeeded; and the glory of Europe is extinguished forever.* —Edmund Burke on the French Revolution

Even if you are pretty hazy on the French Revolution, you can recognize that this is the kind of conviction that gets a reader's juices flowing. However, there's a problem: unqualified opinions are often conspicuously wrong. The claim on Irish cigarette packages that "Smokers Die Young" will scare some smokers into quitting, but it will cause others to remember their Uncle Sean who still puffs two packs a day at age eighty-three.

Phrase your opinion so that it is direct without being arrogant, reasonable without being wimpy. Express three times an idea you feel strongly about: once so it is cocksure and irritating, a second time so it is wishy-washy and boring, and a third time so it is both palatable and engaging.

Example:

1. *Dogmatic:* The government's support of the arts, in reality, celebrates untalented, obscene anarchists who are playing the taxpayers for suckers. (dogmatic opinion, loaded language)

2. *Wimpy:* Occasionally, the government may provide public funds for an artist whose work and persona are to some extent outside the norm. (highly qualified opinion, vague language)

3. *Reasonable:* A few government grants have gone to artists who are harsh, even obnoxious, in their criticism of the status quo. Question: should taxpayers be called on to advance the art of those whose taste and morals most people find objectionable? (moderately qualified opinion, moderate language)

8. Look for the Reason

In a discussion, listen for "because" and its synonyms "as," "thanks to," "that's why"—words and phrases like that. It's these links between statements and reasons that are at the core of argument.

This does not mean that every "because" statement is worth a fight. No one is likely to dispute, "It would be a bad idea for me to go to the movies *because* I have too much homework," or "I think the bus will be late this morning *because* a major accident is blocking three lanes of traffic."

But other times "because" signals a more or less wild guess: "Saddam Hussein invaded Kuwait *because* he was trying to compensate for his unhappy childhood."

Working with several other people, brainstorm reasons for each of the following puzzling phenomena. Then write a paragraph explaining and illustrating your claim.

1. People join cults because ...
2. Some people fall in love with convicted serial killers because ...
3. In general, girls get better grades than boys in English because ...
4. People like to stare at fires because ...
5. Dictatorship has been a more common form of government than democracy because ...
6. Children are more likely than adults to laugh at slapstick comedy because ...
7. People collect things like beer mugs, ash trays, and ceramic dolls because ...
8. Some people are afraid of insects because ...
9. Men are more likely than women to watch professional football because ...

Listen to and read other people opinions. Ask yourself, "What are the reasons?"

Essay

The Power of Because: The Logic of Sentences

IF I were Education Czar of the Universe, students would still be diagramming sentences. Well, maybe not in English class. Try art class. Few visual displays communicate more beauty and order and more insight into the accomplishments of the human species than a lovingly diagrammed ornate sentence from, say, Thomas Jefferson. The rendering of restrictive clauses, noun phrases, and indirect objects—each with its own little stem, all connected—can be breathtaking in its complex simplicity.

But for now, we also have some useful, if less classic, techniques for encouraging students to look at how a sentence works. You can illustrate what happens to some sentences when the subordinate conjunction "because" is moved from one clause to the other:

- Because garlic makes people feel sexy, it is in great demand.
- Because garlic is in great demand, it makes people feel sexy.
- Because there are so few bathrooms in this school, students develop strong bladders.
- Because students have strong bladders, there are few bathrooms in this school.

While at least one of the pair of clauses may appear whacky, the right clauses in the hands of an imaginative writer present creative opportunities:

Because my Winter Ball photograph looks funny, I am depressed. You know me; I'm usually full of laughs, but not today. Today I just got those pictures. No, you can't see them, and tonight they will be burned, but I will tell you about them. To start with, my nose is running and my eyes are closed. My corsage juts at a weird angle, and my dress, which my mother made me wear, looks like it is about to fall off. My date is wearing an expression that suggests he has just smelled a dirty sock, and he is grabbing me like a linebacker trying to bring down Marcus Allen. Now, tell me, if that were your picture, wouldn't you be depressed?

Because I am depressed, my Winter Ball photograph looks funny. *I may very well resemble Morgan Fairchild in these photographs, but that's not the way I see them today. It's hard to be objective about a picture on the day your alarm goes off at four when you intend to sleep until seven, when you find bugs crawling in your breakfast cereal, when your mother tells you must take care of your little brother all weekend, when you flunk a chemistry test, and when all you have to look forward to after school is an orthodontist appointment. Faced with circumstances like these, a mere Winter Ball picture is not going to be much of an upper.*

Ask students to fool around with a complex sentence, making one clause subordinate, then the other. They can then use each of these statements as a topic sentence, as in the student model above.

9. Develop Standards for Your Critical Opinions

Think about the criteria you use to decide that a certain movie comedy is fabulous, lame, terrific, or dorky. Get behind the judgmental words: What do you expect in a movie comedy?

Spell out your criteria for judging some of the following. At their best, what qualities do they have?

- a hamburger
- a rock group
- ice cream
- a supermarket
- a musical video
- a dentist
- a soap opera
- a teacher
- an automobile
- a fast food restaurant
- a perfect weekend
- a politician

After you've developed your criteria for judgment, pick an example that meets your specifications and explain why. The examples which follow, both nominating a different best second-hand clothing store in San Francisco, appeared in the student publication, *The Best of Teenage San Francisco*. What criteria do the writers share? How do they differ? Note, in both pieces, the numerous supporting specifics.

1.

Held Over is the place to buy second-hand clothes. This Haight Street store offers a wide variety of clothing from tennis shoes and argyle socks to top hats and bow ties. You can find an outfit for a costume party or a prom, for work or for play.

Unlike most second-hand stores, Held Over offers quality clothes at very reasonable prices. If you do find a hole in a cashmere sweater, you can usually get the price lowered from the already low $12.95.

The store is clean, organized and spacious. You never will see a pair of Bermuda shorts on the carpeted floor or hanging with the Hawaiian shirts. Because the clothes are separated by sizes within their own sections, you won't need to search through all the Army pants to find the ones that fit you. Since Held Over is a large and uncluttered store, there is room to walk around without bumping into another customer. Although everything should be easy to find, three or four workers are always around to help you find the pinstriped suit you've been looking for.

Held Over is easy to reach by car or bus...

2.

Walk past the nude mannequins, under the ornate chandelier that hangs from the high ceiling and stop before the New Wave couch. All around you are high brick walls covered with blow-ups of Cary Grant, John Lennon, and other superstars. Roman pillars pretend to support the ceiling. You are surrounded by aluminum racks from which hang the rags of a nation.... Welcome to American Rags.

American Rags, a second-hand clothing store at 1355 Bush Street, is not for everyone. It does not have the latest styles as seen in Vogue *or* GQ, *but prides itself on clothes that come with history and personality ready to blend with and accent your own.*

Each section of the store is devoted to a different type of clothes. "Uniformly Elegant" carries Navy jackets and sailor tops, parachuting suits, camouflage pants, and heavy wool coats for those times the fog roles in. "Warhol on Wall Street" and "Ol' Sport" group men's suits by materials and colors: green seersucker, mauve hound's tooth, plaid oxford, even a set of aquamarine blazers with Jefferson Acappella Choir patches. "Smart Kids" displays shirts and shorts for the young and small in body.

There are leather jackets and glamorous wool sweaters that will make you look like a character out of a James Bond movie. There are also party dresses in ruffles, feathers, lace and beads, woven Indian tops, and paisley vests.

Along the back wall are curtained dressing rooms and several enormous mirrors. Elsewhere, showcases hold small treasures like ties, felt hats, gloves, fake but expensive looking jewelry, even baby shoes.

For a second-hand clothing store, American Rags is amazingly clean: straight rows of clothes, a hangerless floor, and sparking glass. Everywhere, the workers, capable of giving constructive criticism and helpful ideas, are confident and well dressed.

American Rags. Check it out.

Bad Signs Can Make Good Inferences

KIDS love the feeling that they are learning from their experience. It is a sign they are growing up. A "snap judgment" may not necessarily spring from a prejudice, but rather may be a seasoned opinion motivated by one too many hard knocks.

I enjoy sharing with my students ways I can tell a mediocre restaurant before I ever sample the food.

- They put you at the bar even though you have a reservation.
- They have a public address system that blares, "Jones, party of two, your table is ready."
- They pipe in Muzak—or whatever it's called now.
- The napkins are rolled up and placed in the wine glasses.
- The maitre d' announces "Your waitperson tonight will be Debbie."
- Debbie is costumed as a serving wench.

On the other hand, any of these negative observations can be offset by a predominant aroma of garlic.

Ask students to detail clues that let them know:

- the movie is going to be bad
- a girlfriend or boyfriend is losing interest
- a new teacher is going to be uptight or spacy
- it's the wrong time to ask their parents to borrow the car
- a party is going to be boring.

10. Use Facts Creatively

The same fact can serve different, even opposite, arguments depending on its interpretation and context.

Here's Garrison Keillor testifying before a congressional committee looking into the National Endowment for the Arts funding: *We've heard three or four times this morning that, of 85,000 works funded by the N.E.A., only twenty were controversial. I don't know why anyone would cite that as something to be proud of.*

One fact. Opposite interpretations.

Here is some practice choosing data which serves your purpose. Below is a list of facts about men and women. Suppose your goal is to (a) undermine stereotypes associated with the sexes or (b) defend traditional sex roles or (c) argue the superiority (physical, intellectual, or moral) of one sex over the other.

Find the facts that serve your purpose. Explain how they help. The *how* is important as some of the same facts may be put to more than one purpose, and others may be of no use at all.

The Facts:

- A female executive is about twenty times more likely to be single or divorced than a male executive.
- Twice as many males as females age twenty-five to twenty-nine live with their parents.
- Thirty-six percent of husbands but only nineteen percent of wives say that sometimes their spouses are like gods to them.
- There are 29,000 female prisoners and 553,000 male prisoners in state and federal prisons.
- Women are over three times more likely than men to say they prefer a male boss to a female.
- On the average, men and women walk at almost exactly the same speed per minute.

- More women than men say their biggest thrill would be to get the winning hit in the World Series.
- There are twenty clinically diagnosed male sexual masochists for every female.
- In the classrooms of coed colleges, male students are more than twice as likely to speak as female students.
- Twice as many women as men think that hunting and killing animals for sport is unacceptable.
- In books that won the Caldecott Medal for excellence in children's books, ten boys are pictured for every girl.
- Twenty percent of women follow horse racing, as opposed to seventeen percent of males.
- About three times more males than females (sixty-eight percent to twenty-two percent) like the way they look in the nude.
- Male stutterers outnumber female stutterers three to one.
- When they get depressed, females are about twice as likely (fifty-eight percent to twenty-nine percent) to call a friend.

Source: Daniel Evanweiss, *The Great Divide*. New York, Poseidon Press, 1991.

11. Be Careful with Opinions That Link Facts

If it's a fact that event A happened and then event B happened, it's not always a fact that A caused B. Be cautious with opinions that express these causal connections. Your reader will be judging whether your conjecture is rooted in evidence, a wild guess or a creative speculation. How convincing are each of the following pieces of cause-effect conjecture?

Fact A: During World War II, many American soldiers stationed in Italy learned to enjoy pizza and the oregano that often came as part of it.

Fact B: In the decade after the War, there was a 5,200 percent jump in U.S. oregano sales.

A caused **B.**

Fact A: Cher won an Academy Award.

Fact B: The next week, Cher's ex-husband Sonny Bono was elected mayor of Palm Springs.

A caused **B.**

Fact A: In 1987, the TV show "LA Law" debuted.

Fact B: In 1988, there was a twenty-two percent increase in students taking the law school admission exam.

A caused **B.**

Fact A: In the 1950s, Davy Crockett, the TV hero of millions of children, wore buckskin and a raccoon tail hat and, at the Alamo, refused to budge.

Fact B: In the 1960s, many college students grew ponytails (not unlike raccoon tails) wore buckskin, and made non-negotiable demands on college administrators.

A was a cause of **B.**

Try some conjectures about your own history. Consider, in chronological sequence, major changes in your life. What was the cause of each? Try to anchor both the cause and the effect in specific events.

Not:

A. My high-school boyfriend became distant and inattentive.

B. I broke up with him at the end of my junior year.

A caused **B.**

Rather:

A. My high-school boyfriend went to the Demolition Derby with his buddies on the night of the Junior Prom.

A. At intimate moments, he kept calling me Wanda. My name is Jane.

B. I broke up with him at the end of my junior year.

Incidents such as **A** caused **B.**

Another Example:

A. My little sister was born.

A. My mother went back to work.

B. I began to feel lonely.

A was a cause of **B.**

Deconstruction 1A: Rookie Interpreters Take Their Cuts

STUDENTS love the J.C. Principle. The J.C. Principle asserts that when a character with the initials J.C. appears in a literary work, it is likely that this character is a stand-in for Jesus Christ. Kids are attracted to this and other neat explanations, treating them with a level of certainty more properly reserved for Newton's Third Law of Motion.

Some teachers are tempted to play to this vulnerability, to let kids in on the literary inside dope. Have they heard? Huck and Jim are latent homosexuals. "The Tempest" is really about American foreign policy since World War II. And anything red stands for sex.

Increasingly, however, I've found it important to counter the notion that interpretations must come fully assembled and ready to plug in. I want to push students toward making rather than regurgitating meaning, toward original interpretation supported by the text. No longer would I consider inappropriate, as I once did, a student essay which began, "Like a lot of young adults before and since, Hamlet finds his problems getting worse when his mom marries a jerk." Using the language of the play as evidence, the writer went on to parallel Hamlet's situation and his own.

Students should understand that interpretation, literary and otherwise, has less to do with arriving at Ultimate Truth than with manipulating ideas. Kids should be let in on the fun. They should be encouraged to think of interpretation as an intellectual game to which they may bring their powers of imagination and creativity. To illustrate the possibilities in inventing meaning, I draw on models from a collection which ranges from the brilliant to the bizarre—sometimes the brilliantly bizarre.

Here are some:

- One psychoanalyst looks at Christmas morning gift exchanges: *Christmas gift-giving is a ritual enactment of childbirth—with prepa-*

ration symbolizing pregnancy, the rush to open presents an expression of labor, opening the gifts as childbirth and the showing off of one's new possessions an equivalent to showing off a new child.

- During the last days of the Cold War, believers in the literal truth of the Book of Revelations made Mikhail Gorbachev out to be the Anti-Christ by employing the following intellectual pyrotechnics: *The Anti-Christ will appear abruptly; Gorbachev emerged abruptly. He'll have seven heads. That would have been the seven Warsaw pact nations. He'll have ten horns: the ten nations the Soviet Union had devoured. His feet will be those of a bear. Remember the bear symbol of the Soviet Union? He will be the eighth king of a country. Gorbachev was eighth in a line of rulers starting from Lenin.*

- Professor Umberto Eco interprets the cathartic effect of the "Peanuts" comic strip: *The poetry of these children is born from the fact that we find in them all the sufferings of adults who remain offstage. These children affect us because in a certain sense they are monsters: They are the monstrous infantile reductions of all the neuroses of a modern citizen of the industrial age. Suddenly in the encyclopedia of contemporary weaknesses, there are, as we have said, luminous patches of light, free variations, allegros and rondos where all is pacified in a few bars. The monsters turn into children again. (Charles) Schulz becomes only a poet of childhood.*

- University of California Professor Allan Dundes interprets the ancient flood myth: *The ancient story of a worldwide flood that destroys the earth and begins the human race anew represents a sacred charter for male domination over females. ... The global flood is a symbol of urination, the male approximation of the amniotic fluid that gushes from the uterus at birth.*

- Some interpretations business writers John Clemens and Douglas Mayer put forward in *The Classic Touch — Lessons in Leadership from Homer to Hemingway:* Shakespeare's *King Lear* portrays an aging executive trying to decide when to give up power. Sophocles' *Antigone* is the story of a boss who rejects a suggestion from an underling and, therefore, finds himself alone and headed for disaster when it turns out Antigone is right.

- The movie *E.T.* is, according to theologian Robert Short, a retelling of the life of Jesus. E.T. came from a mysterious beyond; the establishment disbelieved and rejected him, yet he was innocent of any wrong; he performed miracles, died, lived again and ascended.

- Samuel Beckett once said of his play, *Waiting for Godot,* that it was about him and his wife arguing.

Presented with these examples of adults making meaning with all the vigor of kids constructing sand castles, students come to understand that the teacher's answer book is not necessarily the guide to The Right Answer. Given these models, some students are able to come up with fanciful interpretations of Little Red Riding Hood, April Fool's Day, or The Academy Award Ceremony. Most students, however, need to start more slowly, as with the following workout which encourages alternative explanations of facts.

12. Consider Alternative Explanations

An explanation is often a kind of opinion. Don't be in a hurry to insist on a single explanation for every fact or observation you encounter. Here's what can happen:

Fact: Twenty years ago, it took two people to carry home ten dollar's worth of groceries. Today any five-year-old can do it.

Explanation: Like I've always said, every year Americans are getting stronger.

Yes, the starlet who makes several trips to the bathroom during a Hollywood party may be spooning cocaine, but then again she could have eaten some bad oysters.

Here are some facts. In each case suggest at least two explanations.

- Only six percent of those quoted in the *New York Times* front page stories are women.
- Most bank robberies occur on Friday.
- The suicide rate among dentists is far higher than in the population at large.
- Jane Fonda wore the same dress to the Academy Awards two years in a row.
- The per capita sale of *Playboy* magazine in Des Moines is almost three times what it is in New York City.
- Sixty percent of American men say they would not have sex with Madonna if she asked them.
- Mothers talk more to baby girls than to baby boys.
- In jealousy killings, the loved one rather than the rival is more likely to end up dead.
- Of the four military services, the Navy has historically had the highest desertion rate.
- The musical group Toto received six Grammy Awards. This contrasts with the Beatles who received four Grammy Awards.

13. Keep Your Facts Relevant to Your Opinion

When you are developing an argument, make sure your facts are in sync with the opinion you wish to advance. Sure, it's true that boxing has given a lot of feisty kids an opportunity to get out of the ghetto, but this fact does not answer the claim that since boxing is such a dangerous sport it should be banned.

Below are a series of facts. Integrate one of them in a paragraph which adds relevant support to an opinion.

Example:

Fact: Humphrey Bogart once said, "I made more lousy pictures than any actor in history."

Irrelevant use: *Some of the most entertaining Hollywood films are among the industry's worst artistic products. Pia Zadora's "Santa Claus Conquers the Martians" benefits from a cosmic silliness lacking altogether in "Citizen Kane." We do not give enough credit to Hollywood androids, maniacs on the loose, and lovesick vampires. More attention should be paid to the movie that is so bad it is good. Even Humphrey Bogart admitted,* **"I made more lousy pictures than any actor in history."**

Relevant use: *One usually grows in stature by admitting his or her limitations. When that now forgotten performer, Pat Boone, confesses "There's something about me that makes a lot of people want to throw up," he becomes more, not less, likable. Humphrey Bogart may claim,* **"I made more lousy pictures than any actor in history,"** *but when he says this, we are reminded not so much of his bad movies as the films made better by his presence. When (former) British Prime Minister Margaret Thatcher—the Iron Maiden—admits she "never had the figure for jeans," she leaves us surprised and impressed that she would give a moment's thought to such a picayune deficiency.*

Write an opinion paragraph making relevant use of one of the following facts:

- Many of Freud's most influential ideas were conceived during the period in which he was addicted to cocaine.
- Both Hitler and Mao Zedong were vegetarians.
- Karl Marx, the most famous critic of industrial capitalism, never set foot in a factory.
- No one knows for sure where Mozart is buried.
- The blood washing down the drain in *Psycho* was actually made of chocolate sauce.
- Mohammed is the most common name in the world.
- George Washington's face was badly scarred by small pox.
- Babe Ruth, one of the greatest hitters of all time, began his career as a pitcher.
- The most commonly used word in conversation is "I."

PART IV: WRITERS CONSIDER OTHER PEOPLE

- "Has Anyone Here Ever ... ?":
  Nine Ways to Connect with Your Reader

- Leading the Prose Dance:
  *Three Techniques for Meeting Your
  Reader's Expectations*

Classroom Audiences

THE workouts in this section focus on the relationship between writers and their audiences. Audience (as in, "It's great to be back in Duluth. What an audience!") is not a word most people associate with writing. However, while it is true that a writer's audience may not be measured by Nielson & Associates, Inc., writers who are read usually do think of their readers. Student writers don't often make the connection between school writing and writing to be read. Yet most classrooms are full of enough audiences to rival a shopping mall multiplex.

Teachers as Audience

I remember the sentence: "Juke box John Coltrane arpeggios giant-stepped through the thick blue smoke." No, its author was not some retro-beatnik poet. Rather, this sentence was written by Lisa, a self-described "girl-nerd," best known among her classmates for her tendency to raise the average on calculus exams. Lisa had embedded these words in a piece responding to one of those assignments that make big city teaching a special pleasure: Go to a location where you have never been and would normally not go and describe the setting. Her location was the Blue Monkey Cafe where the conversation runs more to postmodern theory than to functions and logarithms.

How did I react to her sentence? I tingled. I knew nothing of Lisa's out-of-school life. But I did not expect I would have much in common with a person who derived such great pleasure from casting out nines. With one sentence that changed. The girl not only knew of Coltrane, the sainted post-bopster, she had transformed his seminal composition—Giant Steps—into a verb!

Lisa—maybe, inadvertently—had spoken to her audience: me. From that moment on, I felt a little rush of anticipation whenever her paper surfaced in the pile that contained my weekly diet of student essays. Such is the power generated by connecting with a reader.

Classmates as Audience

"Please do not make me read this in front of the class."

Almost all teachers have seen papers with this usually hastily appended request. Often the writer does not want to spotlight some personal trauma—a family drinking problem, a bitter argument with a friend. I find these requests touching, if a little bewildering. I am moved that the student would share this intimacy with me, but wonder what kind of oaf would drag a student before a class to lay out the grimy details. I suppose this request usually is just a way of saying, "I am letting you in on a secret."

Sometimes, however, "Please do not make me read this ... " has another motivation: the fear of being unpopular, a dread that has probably provoked more teenage anxiety than any threat short of loss of The Driving Privilege.

One such communiqué came from Kristen, a Molly Ringwald look-alike. She was smart, funny, and considerate. She had a boyfriend, and, so it seemed, several dozen other admirers waiting in the wings. She was the kind of person who could make a dent in the biases of her peers, and her paper was an argument for allowing same sex couples to attend the prom.

Intrigued, I asked, "Won't you read this?"

"Come on, I just wrote this for a grade," she said, blushing slightly. "I didn't even show it to my group. People won't like it. They'll think I'm gay."

I decided to respect her wishes and go at this from another angle. I asked my classes to write anonymously a paragraph on the question, "Should same sex couples be allowed to attend the prom?" Kristen's position won, though not by much.

"No comment," she said.

About a year later I received from Kristen a copy of an essay she had written for college freshman English. It was an expanded version of the paper she had done for my class, now titled "Girls and Girls Together: Why Not?" Among other comments the teacher had written, "The class would be interested in hearing these ideas."

Kristen had appended her own one sentence note, writing, "I read it!"

As they say, college is liberating.

Students as a Tough Audience

Of course, I am distressed when I begin to hear the classroom white noise, the barely audible whispered conversations about hot cars and cold teachers that are competing with my enthusiastic presentation on the nature of restrictive clauses. But these murmurs are sweet music indeed compared to the saddest of all classroom sounds: total and eerie silence except for my own disembodied voice droning incessantly about how every educated person should have read blah-blah-blah. Now, before my unseeing eyes, thirty-one sixteen-year-olds have either died or transported themselves to another dimension.

On one such occasion, optimistically assuming the latter, I stop abruptly. I raise my voice: "Hold it!" thirty-one necks whiplash to attention.

"Please take out a paper and write down what you were just thinking about." Six students, rightfully sensing an invasion of their personal space and their Fifth Amendment rights, refuse to participate. Of the twenty-five who comply, several are probably making it up as they go along. Still, I keep these scraps of paper as a reminder that the term "captive audience" refers only to bodies, not minds, and—in the case of libidinous teenagers—maybe not even bodies. Here's a sample from my collection:

- I was figuring out what would be my grade-point average if I get a "D" in this class.

- I was listening to you the way I always listen to all my teachers (Heh, Heh).
- I sang this song to myself, but I'm sure you wouldn't know it or ever have heard it.
- How I'm going to tell my mom if she wants me to be in all these activities and get good grades and everything I can't pick up my brother after school all the time.
- I had this mental picture of Jerry and how FINE he looks in his 501s.
- I was remembering a dream I had where this teacher in the P.E. department whose name I don't know was asking me to dance at this club where I've never been.
- I was thinking about if I could get away with finishing my math homework here, which I have next period. But I didn't want to hurt your feelings.
- I said over and over to myself "hedgy pen, hedgy pen coup lac." This is something I do when I get very bored. It works!!
- S-E-X (CENSORED) S-E-X (CENSORED) MORE S-E-X.
- I was wondering how this English will help me get a job.
- What goes into falafel? My boyfriend gave me some at lunch, but I don't think he knows.

Reading these now-public private thoughts, I am struck by the distressing recognition that, unlike the stand-up comic passing through Duluth, I will be right back here with the same audience tomorrow. I had better get my act together.

"Has Anyone Here Ever ... ?": Nine Ways to Connect with Your Reader

1. Picture Your Reader

If you are writing for someone other than yourself, focus on that person, real or imagined. Invite him or her to read over your shoulder. Find the ritual that works:

> *When I write I aim my mind ... toward a vague spot a little to the east of Kansas. I think of the books on library shelves, without their jackets, years old, and a countryish teenage boy finding them and having them speak to him.*
> —John Updike

or:

> *The ideal reader of my novels is a lapsed Catholic and failed musician, shortsighted, color-blind, auditorily based, who has read the books I have read. He should also be about my age.*
> —Anthony Burgess

Imagine and describe the appearance, habits, and values of the reader of the following:

- your resume for your dream job
- your personal ad (think about the ideal reader)
- your letter of complaint (make this real, consider a time you have, in fact, been ripped off or badly treated)
- your letter to the editor of a specialized magazine you read (you may picture someone who will read the published letter, rather than the editor)
- your college application essay.

Describe other possible readers for specific pieces of writing.

Comment

Of course, plenty of writers of literature claim they write only for themselves, or "for the page" as I once heard one very serious practitioner put it. Should students be encouraged to "write for themselves?" Of course. Particularly if they are their own primary readers. Self-contemplation comes easily to sixteen-year-olds, and writing to oneself about life's challenges and puzzles promotes sanity.

But students need to know that writing is more than a tool for self-discovery; it is also a way of being discovered, of putting a face forward to other people. With every sentence writers have the power to attract, convince, or irritate a reader, sometimes all at the same time.

One way I encourage this perspective is to ask students to find a word, a sentence a paragraph, an entire essay to which someone they know would react, positively or negatively. Some examples:

- *I think my junior high school art teacher would like the second sentence here. "In the Financial District, at this time of morning, the streets are empty except for a few garbage trucks. The Trans-America building is different shades of purple." She was always telling us, "Color is light."*

- *My father lives in another town and I don't think he has a lot of confidence in me. A couple of years ago he saw the movie "Slacker," and he's made some remarks about how I might fit right in with the people in that movie. I'd like him to read this essay which explains some of the things I'd like to do with my life.*

2. Be Polite

Don Rickles, Howard Stern, Ice-T, and Rush Limbaugh aside, you are not going to change many minds by calling another person a hockey puck—or worse. Unless you have a high-visibility performance venue and a big-bucks publicity agent to smooth things over, rhetorical bad manners are not an asset, and will embarrass even your friends. Better to discard the "you're a moron, I'm a genius" argument style and try to be civil. Here's some practice.

State three or more positive habits, character traits or motives of a person with whom you disagree on an issue close to you. The issue need not be a global one, but may be one related to work, school, neighborhood, social life, or family.

Keep the praise more or less related to the issue.

3. Climb into Your Reader's Skin

Pick a real or imagined person with whom you disagree on a particular issue: a parent who doesn't want you to work at a part-time job, a student who dresses entirely in black on school Color Day, someone who opposes or favors prayers in the school. Write a first-person account of the real or imagined circumstances that may have led to that person's belief.

Example:

The following monologue was written by an adult who was having trouble understanding why "anyone would be for school vouchers." Then she imagined a character and cast her in real-life events:

I'm a single mother, two kids eight and twelve, renting a one-bedroom apartment, supporting the three of us on my clerical job at an insurance company. I never finished high school and I believe in the importance of a good education. But almost everyday my kids come home with stories about something horrible that happened at school: three more students added to a fourth grade class of thirty-eight; a crack bust on the middle school playground; the young teacher who had turned my daughter on to science resigning abruptly and in tears, driven out by unruly students and a weak administration. Now the government comes along and offers me an education voucher so I can send my kids to any school I choose, just like the rich folks.

4. Remind Your Reader of Shared Experience

You are connecting with readers when they say, "Hey that happened to me." Readers pay attention when you remind them of the dumb questions they have been asked at job interviews and the monopoly prices they are charged at movie snack bars. Here Ellen Goodman writes of an irritation shared by thousands.

> *It is 3 A.M., a happy hour for creatures of the deep REM, the time of night when pillow and posture have found their natural resting state and the mind is free to dream. But somewhere from the middle distance, a sound is piercing the plotline of one urban sleeper's dream.*
>
> *WAAAH. One long loathsome note in the night. It is the well-known cry from the modern beast of burden, the car alarm.*
>
> *Behind a brick wall our sleeper gradually and reluctantly is roused from the kingdom of deep REM. One eye opens onto the green numbers of the digital clock: 3:15 A.M.*
>
> *She is a veteran of many such nights in a city where car alarms are more common than cat howls...*
>
> —Ellen Goodman

Pick a phenomena that commonly generates aggravation. Think about the specifics of your own experience with this unpleasantness. However, attribute your experience to a third person as Goodman does when she presents what may have happened to her as happening to an "urban sleeper."

Special Interests: Understanding Cultural Literacies

BEING around kids keeps me young." I've used this slice of cocktail party small talk ever since I was—well—young.

Now, even as the mirror offers convincing evidence to the contrary, I still feel that teaching has left me with a spunk that might not have survived had I been an accountant.

But being around teenagers has also made me feel old. Often these fits of unplanned obsolescence develop over clashes in our understanding of language. The problem isn't their language. I leave kids alone to "dis" their "dweebs," or whatever. I have plenty of grownup synonyms for "rad." The problem is my language. I have zillions of examples, all small, but the cumulative effect is distressing.

On one occasion, I am driving a carload of fourteen-year-olds back from a class camping trip. For hours they are engaged in wall-to-wall chatter and I am tuned out and sulking. I know that any effort on my part to mount Mozart on the tape deck will not be greeted with enthusiasm. I am mentally kicking myself for caving in without even trying.

About two hours into the ride a cheerleader-type notices my stony face. "You're not saying much, Mr. P.," she chirps.

"I guess I'm just not ready for all this togetherness," I say sardonically. A two-beat pause, the chatter resumes—without me.

Now I am really sulking. Of course, they did not hear the quotation marks around "togetherness." They are thinking all I mean is "to be together." Of course, they are not thinking The Age of Conformity, The Man in the Gray Flannel Suit, I Like Ike, and The Power of Positive Thinking.

I am not going to interrupt their bubbling for a pedantic explanation of the connotations of "togetherness," that it had to do with picket fences and stay-at-home moms preparing tuna casseroles. I could tell them that those of us who didn't like Ike found such a concept "stifling." But these kids, living in an era when it's hard to round up a quorum for Thanksgiving dinner, would have good reason to consider such a perspective arrogant and twisted. Maybe it was. Certainly Ike is looking better all the time.

The point here is that, unlike adults who work exclusively with other adults, teachers are reminded regularly not so much of their mortality as of their anachronism.

My sensitivity to this cross-generational illiteracy is one reason I developed the following workout. It's a way of reminding writers of what they already know but, in practice, too often forget: Readers bring with them different experiences and knowledge; the person who remembers the day Glen Miller's plane went down may not be up on the fine points of "The Rocky Horror Picture Show." And vice versa.

---

5. Think about What Your Reader Doesn't Know

One way to scare off a reader is to assume the reader knows things he or she, in fact, doesn't know. A reader who constantly must wonder "who's he?" and "what's that?" is not likely to stay around. Yet many writers—and speakers, too—plow ahead, oblivious. There was, for instance, the time ex-British Prime Minister and former chemist Margaret Thatcher was visiting a London slum school trying to explain the principle of oxidation: "Think what happens when you eat an egg with a silver spoon," she said. The eyes glazed over.

The story goes that high-school kids in the mid-1980s, on seeing in print the name "Malcolm X," would sometime ask their teachers, "So who is this Malcolm the Tenth?" No longer, of course.

Keep tuned to what your reader knows and doesn't know. Consider this list of words, a few of which are up with the times, some of which are past their prime, and others of which are someplace in between. How many of these terms can you explain? Don't be surprised if you know only a few. That's the way it will be for most people. Then pick two people you know who have a lot of differences, including age, education, and interests. Ask them about these words. Record what they say.

The List

- air guitar
- all-day sucker
- The Summer of Love
- mushroom cloud
- the grassy knoll
- bra burner
- dashiki
- mommy track
- to chill out
- hawks and doves
- lollapalooza
- rave

- wash day
- blush wine
- BLT
- SDS
- slasher flick
- Eliot Ness
- hyperspace
- cyberpunk
- blitzkrieg
- butterfingers
- voguing
- sampling

- Statue of Liberty play
- ouija board
- slacker
- brinkmanship
- The Quiz Kids
- The New Look
- headbanger
- streaking
- Yippie (not Yuppie)
- gravy train
- fly girl

Now, ask the people you interview to talk more about the language of their generation, the words that are special to people in their age group. Write two paragraphs contrasting the responses of your two subjects.

Some of these words—lollapalooza and fly girl, for instance—will have very different meanings for different generations.

A goal of this workout is to encourage writers to ask, "Is my reader likely to know what I am talking about?" and then, "Do I want her to understand?" and "Should I explain?"

Essay

You Live in an Alternative Universe? Hey, No Problem!

EVEN though I encourage students to keep in mind what their readers know, erudite generational allusions in student writing have not always been a problem for me. When I find myself bewildered by a writer's reference, I am also often intrigued by its specificity.

Specialized language is frequently used more to create an effect than to give information. Once, describing a concert he attended, a student wrote of taking "an attack dose of Piracetam," a scary and alien-sounding phrase. Later, when I asked the eighteen-year-old about it, he gave a James Dean shrug and said, "It's OK, it's a smart drug." He noticed, I think, that I did not find this information particularly comforting and that suited him just fine. He was not applying for Eagle Scout, and he had achieved the effect he wanted.

6. Imagine Your Reader's Questions

Step back from your work and ask questions as though you were a reader.

- What kind of person could remember, what's more describe, all the hair styles she has had in her life?
- OK. You're making our hearts bleed for the tough lives of the criminals. How about the victims?
- Why should I care that the National League strike zone seems to grow a little each year?

Here's a way to practice a conversation with a reader. Think of a group you support that needs money. Write a letter to a possible donor soliciting a donation. Be passionate and specific as you enumerate the organization's present and future good works. Now read your letter over, looking for places a reader might say, "Wait a minute…" What is your reader thinking? How can you answer?

Comment

One way to help some students imagine their reader's questions as they revise, but not before, is to ask them to allow a curious, intelligent, and imaginary talking parrot on their shoulder. As they write, the bird will persist in asking questions and making comments. They can give the bird a name, a color, an attitude.

Once or twice a semester I'll ask students to show me a second draft of a paper in which this parrot is speaking up. Here is part of what "Bonaparte" had to say to Melissa Kung about a research paper she was writing on the music of the 1960s:

> *The musicians of the 1960s were more socially conscious than the musicians of today. (B: **You are forgetting U-2?**) One group, Country Joe and the Fish, who wrote the protest song*

"Fixin' to Die Rag," did a lot to turn teenagers and college students against the war in Viet Nam. (B: Are you sure they weren't already against the war? Also is this the same Country Joe who led the obscene "Fish Cheer?"—"Give me an F," etc. Are you going to tell me about that? You think he's a good example?) *Protest singer Woody Guthrie's son, Arlo, wrote a song against the draft in his very popular composition "Alice's Restaurant."* (B: Alice's Restaurant? That doesn't sound like a protest song. Please explain.)

I like this form as more than just an exercise in dialogue with the reader. Even as the questions are asked and not answered, a tension is created which is a feature of much good writing.

7. Intrigue with a Title

You can hook an uncommitted reader with an engaging title. Of course, some subjects are easier to enliven in this way than others. The writer of the headline "NEW HOPE FOR THE DEAD" has a lot more to work with than the one who must report "NEPAL PREMIER WON'T RESIGN."

Effective titles may be disorienting, thus intriguing:
The Day the Lampshades Breathed —Ed McClanahan
Save the Whales, Screw the Shrimp —Joy Williams
Waiter There's a Paragraph in My Soup —Joseph Epstein

Or they may play with words and allusions:
The Median Isn't the Message —Stephen Jay Gould
Portrait of the Artist as a Lion on Stilts —Paul West
Mozart and the Wolf Gang —Anthony Burgess

Or suggest contentiousness:
Why Mow? The Case Against Lawns —Michael Pollan
The Idiocy of Urban Life —Henry Fairlie
On the Pleasure of Being Late —Samuel Pickering

Or promise self revelation:
On My Racism: Notes by a WASP —Henry DeWitt
No Wonder They Call Me a Bitch —Ann Hodgman

Recall the subject matter of one of your generic essays, the kind everyone gets around to writing sometime: "My Most Embarrassing Moment" or "An Event That Changed My Life." Try four new titles for this essay, one from each of the categories above.

8. Snare Your Reader in Your First Paragraph

Think of your opening paragraph as your one chance to grab a fleeting reader by the collar and shout, "Read this!" Here are some ways to suck in a reader:

- **Appeal to Self Interest:** *Who owns who, the dog or the owner? Don't laugh. If you're a dog owner, it's an important question: Who dominates—you or the dog? Dogs are pack animals that have a social hierarchy. They jockey for top dog status. Consequently, veterinarians say the most common canine behavior problem is aggression stemming from a dog's dominant position over people. If you don't master a little dog psychology, you may never become the master of your dog. And the penalty you pay for being the "underdog" is hassles with neighbors, landlords, and family members.* —Barbara Somerville

- **Begin with an Arresting Snatch of Dialogue:** *"I hate buffets; I'm bulimic," Maxine remarks casually, as if she's admitting that purple is her favorite color. We are standing in the buffet line at the Westwood Marquis Hotel, an unlikely choice for a confessional.* —Margo Kaufman

- **Ask an Intriguing Question:** *Do you ever wake up in a panic in the middle of the night and say, "Oh nuts! I forgot to buy some T-shirts!" Do you find yourself saying, "What I need to do today, right now, immediately is buy a scotty-dog refrigerator magnet"? Do you sometimes hear a voice crying, "May I have just one Kiss the Chef Apron before I die?" If the answer to all these questions is a resounding "No, stupid," then explain this: Why are there so many gift shops?* —Alice Kahn

- **Create a Mystery:** *Of the three men in the room, one was bored, one was anxious, and one was dead. The sixty-two-year-old pathologist, heavy set and bald, languidly prepared to make his in-*

cision. I was the anxious one—an intern, age twenty-three, my face stubbled with a three-day growth of beard, my eyes fixed intently on the pathologist's scalpel blade. On the table lay the suntanned body of the patient, age forty-three. —Oscar London

- **Introduce an Idea with a Story:** *A woman and her small son were out walking when they encountered a man who had some oranges. The man offered one of the oranges to the little boy, who snatched it and said nothing.*

    The embarrassed mother said, "Johnny, what do you say to the nice man?"

    Johnny held the orange out and said, "Peel it!"

    Many political movements today are very much like that little boy. It is the age of spoiled brat politics… —Thomas Sowell

- **Defy Readers' Expectations:** *Among the issues at stake on that warm wet evening when Ingemar Johansson and Floyd Patterson stepped into a field of light at Yankee Stadium, the heavyweight championship of the world ranked third."* —Roger Kahn

State a specific opinion you have about an aspect of American culture right now. **Examples:**

- *It is becoming increasingly possible to lead a full life without leaving home.*
- *Recycling, once an environmental buzzword, is becoming a middle-class habit.*
- *Drinking booze now joins smoking cigarettes as a source of social stigma.*

Using this idea, write two separate beginnings modeled on the techniques above.

9. Study Expertly Made Beginnings

Look at the first paragraph of almost any work of fiction. You may notice that it is constructed to leave you wondering. That's often the purpose of an opening: to raise questions about who, what, where, when, why, and how. Here are some first sentences from stories and novels you may have read. What question or questions are raised by each? Can you identify the novel or story?

1. *Dr. Strauss says I should rite down what I think and remembir and evreything that happins to me from now on.*

2. *It was a bright cold day in April and the clocks were striking thirteen.*

3. *Buck did not read the newspapers, or he would have known that trouble was brewing, not alone for himself, but for every tidewater dog, strong of muscle and with warm, long hair, from Puget Sound to San Diego.*

4. *When Gregor Samsa woke up one morning from unsettling dreams, he found himself changed in his bed into a monstrous vermin.*

5. *It was a pleasure to burn.*

6. *In my younger and more vulnerable years my father gave me sane advice that I've been turning over in my mind ever since.*

7. *Mr. Sherlock Holmes, who was usually very late in the mornings, save upon those not infrequent occasions when he was up all night, was seated at the breakfast table.*

8. *There was no possibility of taking a walk that day.*

9. *All children except one, grow up.*

10. *Once upon a time and a very gootime it was there was a moocow coming down along the road and this moocow that was coming down along the road met a nicens little boy named tuckoo…*

Consider an event which has occurred in your life during the last week. Write a sentence about it which should leave a reader wondering.

(The sentence should *not* be a question.) Follow this statement with a paragraph which explains the mysteries of the opening.

Comment

Answers:

1. *Flowers for Algernon* —Daniel Keyes
2. *1984* —George Orwell
3. *Call of the Wild* —Jack London
4. *The Metamorphosis* —Franz Kafka
5. *Fahrenheit 451* —Ray Bradbury
6. *The Great Gatsby* —F. Scott Fitzgerald
7. *The Hound of the Baskervilles* —Arthur Conan Doyle
8. *Jane Eyre* —Charlotte Brontë
9. *Peter Pan* —J. M. Barrie
10. *Portrait of the Artist as a Young Man* —James Joyce

Leading the Prose Dance: Three Techniques for Meeting Your Reader's Expectations

What we've got in this section is pretty much your standard English 1A advice for organizing a piece of writing to conform to what most readers expect. Some writing teachers may suspect that these recommendations come dangerously close to encouraging the five-paragraph essay—a cookie cutter form which, they claim more or less correctly, "does not exist in the real world." But while five-paragraph essays are in short supply outside of classrooms, paragraphs are not. Hundreds of thousands of paragraphs are created everyday, and they are the prime currency in the exchange of written ideas. Competent writers know how to organize a paragraph around a single idea, how to develop it with connected sentences and how to link it to other paragraphs. Readers expect no less.

Let us not forget that in our zeal to get rid of cookie cutters we must still remember how to make cookies.

Essay

A Short History of (My) Paragraph Models

SOMETIMES I feel I have been using paragraph models since about the time Sir Francis Bacon started knocking them out. Models work because in teaching writing, as in writing itself, it is better to show than to tell. The principles of unity, continuity, and development are better illustrated than expounded upon.

The question remains, however, what models? My career as a collector of models has been a checkered one.

By nature, I am drawn to any teaching technique I believe helps students bring order out of chaos. So, in my first year of teaching, I pretty much subscribed to the medical school model of teaching paragraphs. Medical students study basic physiology and anatomy before they study pathology. Likewise, I reasoned, beginning writers need basic paragraph structure before they go all stylistic on us. I was looking for models in which the skeleton was clearly visible, not obscured by layers of complex sentences, figurative language, and complicated detail.

As not many real writers felt obligated to provide me with these industrial strength prose units, I often wrote my own. This was not a particularly difficult task. Here's a typical effort for a junior high school class many years ago:

"The San Francisco Bay Area provides many beautiful things to see, both natural and man-made (topic sentence). The Bay itself is famous the world over as a sight to be admired (first supporting point). As for beauties constructed by human hand (transition), the Golden Gate Bridge is hard to match (second supporting point). No wonder our region attracts so many enthusiastic tourists (clincher)."

Students, also, did not find such paragraphs particularly difficult to write. I'd get back, "My room contains many interesting objects. Some of them are intended for work, others for play. Those that are used for work include … "

After several weeks of this exercise I was going nowhere but crazy. I dreamed one night that I was in my classroom directing my students over and over in the proper way to put on the same nondescript shirt, the same generic trousers, the same government issue shoes. Failure to master this skill, I warned, would lead to arrest for indecent exposure. Meanwhile, outside the classroom, hordes promenaded in hip huggers, culottes, turtlenecks, tank tops, rugby shirts, jackboots, and Docksiders. The symbolism was not lost on me. I began to collect real-life paragraphs written for purposes other than just writing a paragraph, paragraphs that were unified, coherent, developed, *and* zingy. Still the search has not been without complications. Here are three of many paragraphs I have used in recent years.

On the retirement community of Sun City:
Sun Citians keep their homes with fanatical tidiness: the fibers

in the carpets are stiff from vacuuming; the tables reflect one's face. One woman I visited had a plastic runner across her white carpeting; another apologized for the mess in her work room when there was only a pencil and sheet of paper out of place. But the interiors of Sun City homes are not anonymous, for Sun Citians are collectors; their houses are showcases for family treasure and the bric-a-brac collected over a lifetime. On the walls are oil paintings of bucolic landscapes, pastel portraits of children, Thai rubbing, or Chinese lacquer panels inlaid with cherry blossoms. Almost every room has a cabinet filled with pieces of antique and gold-rimmed glass. On the tables are ship models, sports trophies, carved animals, china figurines, or trees made of semi-precious stone. In a week in Sun City, I visited only one house where there was no bric-a-brac to speak of and where the owners lived in a comfortable disarray of newspapers, usable ashtrays, and paperback books. In most Sun City living rooms, the objects seem to rule. China birds, wooden horses, or ivory elephants parade resolutely across coffee tables and seem to have an independent life and purpose of their own.
—Francis Fitzgerald

What I said about this paragraph: Look at the way the details pile up, each supporting the idea that the character of these homes is defined by neatly arranged and very clean objects.

What students said about this paragraph: She shouldn't have written this way about these people after they were nice enough to invite her into their homes.

Has anyone ever noticed that Crosby, Stills and Nash have made a career of reuniting? First it was the No Nukes shows in 1979. Then it was the early-eighties get together that yielded "Southern Cross" and "Wasted on the Way." Then they played Live Aid in 1985. The Bridge Benefit followed a year later. Just last month they reunited again for Farm Aid. Barring a hiatus

for David Crosby's I-was-a-drug-addict-buy-my-book tour, they seem to be reuniting regularly. Sure they haven't toured together in a long time, but with this regular schedule of treasured reunion moments, who could notice?
—Michael MacCambridge

I said: Notice the way the statements of fact are arranged chronologically in support of the topic sentence which is phrased as a question.
They said: Who *are* these people?

There is always the miracle of by-products. Plane a board, the shavings accumulate around your toes ready to be chucked into the stove to kindle your fires (to warm your toes so that you can plane a board.) Draw some milk from a creature to relieve her fullness, the milk goes to the little pig to relieve his emptiness. Drain some oil from a crankcase, and you smear it on the roosts to control the mites. The worm fattens on the apple, the young goose fattens on the worm fruit, the man fattens on the goose, the worm awaits the man. Clean up a barnyard, the pulverized dung from the sheep goes to improve the lawn (before a rain in autumn); mow the lawn next spring, the clippings go to the compost pile, with a few thrown to the baby chickens on the way; spread the composte on the garden and in the fall the original dung, after many vicissitudes, returns to the sheep in the form of an old squash. From the fireplace, at the end of a November afternoon, the ashes are carried to the feet of the lilac bush, guaranteeing the excellence of a June morning.
—E. B. White

I said: Every word supports the concept of "the miracle of by-products." The first examples are simple, followed by detailing of more complex relationships, then returning to the simple and ending with an exhilarating image.
They said: You expect us to do *that?*

As I began to hear this last question more and more, I decided on a new tactic. I would give students more writing I *could* expect them to emulate because it was writing composed by other students. Here, for instance, are three very different paragraphs written by students for very different purposes. All, however, are focused, connected, and unified.

> *Undoubtedly, good manners can be useful. Every politician, for instance, puts manners to his greatest advantage to get what he wants: votes. Smiling, his hand raised and endlessly waving, the politician appears friendly and always mannerly. You'll notice that the politician never pushes or shoves a crowd; instead his body-guards do all the growling and threatening. They are the unmannerly ones. The practical politician knows that if he calls rude members of the press and public nasty names, the public will right away condemn his rudeness and take their support elsewhere. So although many of us may not see eye to eye with many politicians, most of us do respect their "good manners." For a politician, as for the rest of us, it helps to be polite. There is, however, a little problem with good manners: They are boring...*
>
> —Amy Leung, age sixteen

> *I can imagine the editor's office at MacMillan Publishing Company with the WASP male editor on the phone: "Now, Mr. Bragdon, about this new edition of* History of a Free People. *California wants from us four paragraphs about women. It won't sell unless we plug in some stuff about women and minorities. Just come up with something, anything." And that's what we get—anything. Everything seems an afterthought. The section on women in jobs is a barrage of generalizations supported by dead statistics. "Veterans came back from the war and displaced many women in factories. The proportion of women on assembly lines dropped from twenty-five percent in 1944 to seven and a half percent in 1946." The section on Blacks, the section on Puerto Ricans, on Japanese, on*

Native Americans all continue in the same uninteresting prose: shallow generalizations all supported by numbers, numbers, numbers. The writers of such paragraphs clearly have little interest in their subject matter. They must satisfy each special interest that has any political clout. The result is superficial, forced prose. In this book, and other similar ones, references to minorities are tacked on. In one book we get "a Negro cowboy named George McJunkin," in another a "Judge Ming Ramirez." Nothing is developed. Is this how the authors of History of a Free People *intend, as they claim in their prologue, "to promote toleration of different cultures"?*

—June Gin, age eighteen

One of the most valuable lessons my dad has ever taught me was one which required no words. One cold and foggy day five years ago, our family was driving along Highway 1 to the Monterey Bay Aquarium. My dad signaled an impatient motorist behind us to pass, and the driver zoomed by our car. He punctuated his impatience by giving my dad a rather indiscreet display of his third finger through his sunroof. Mistaking the gesture for a wave of thanks, my dad, an immigrant not exactly up on all the nuances of American culture, smiled and waved back to the driver. Presumably baffled by my dad's response, the driver sped off. At that moment the fog seemed to clear and the sun shone through. My dad's reaction left him feeling great. I have taken my dad's misinterpretation and applied it to my life. Whenever life seems to pass by and give me the finger, instead of reacting out of anger or frustration, I try to don a smile and wave back.

—Josephine Tan, age seventeen

1. State Your Claims and Present Your Reasons

In general, readers do not want to have to guess at what a paragraph is up to. Therefore, most forms of writing, most of the time, depend on general statements supported by reasons and evidence.

Here's a way, starting from scratch, to practice this traditional and dominant form—a generalization supported by specifics.

1. Visit a place where there is a lot of activity. It's best if the location is one with which you are not particularly familiar, and, therefore, about which you do not have preconceptions.
2. Focus on individuals. Describe people. Make notes on their actions.
3. Look for an idea that connects some of your observations.
4. State the idea: your topic sentence.
5. Draw on your observations to support this idea.

The following paragraph was written by a high-school student who had made an early morning observation at the school office. From a longer list of observations, she pulled three which she linked with a generalization.

> ***Teachers cannot always leave their private lives at home.*** *In the main office, a P.E. teacher, shuffling impatiently, toying with the whistle about her neck, waits for the phone. Meanwhile a science teacher whose babysitter has failed to show up, walks by the office, his three-year-old son in tow. Moments later the French teacher bursts through the front door, moving at a trot—car trouble again, late again.*
> —Lynn Knapp, age fifteen

2. Begin Each Sentence by Remembering the Previous One

A piece of writing needs to be more than a collection of sentences. The sentences should perform together, sending off a coordinated hum, like the Chicago Bulls moving the ball on a good day.

The following sentences on the next two pages can form a connected paragraph that both explains and demonstrates techniques you can use to hook your sentences together. Use the connecting clues to number the sentences in the order that they would take in a connected paragraph. Sentence "E" is "1." What comes next?

The Connected Paragraph

A. _____ One must, however, be careful not to use an inappropriate connecting word—"therefore" when, for instance, "nevertheless" is needed.

B. _____ So what is a "box" in one sentence becomes a "container" in the next.

C. _____ Problems with another type of link, the repeated word, are more obvious and easier to avoid than pronoun reference problems.

D. _____ One must also approach with caution another type of link, the pronoun.

E. _____ Connections, while not without problems for the writer, are the key to a unified paragraph.

F. _____ To begin with, let's consider the connecting word whose sole function is to show a relationship between what precedes and what follows.

G. _____ Writers who decide they are repeating a word too often may use still another connecting device—the synonym.

H. _____ Attentive writers can hear when they are repeating a word too often.

I. _____ A reader who comes on a pronoun such as "it" or "this" without a clear idea of what the pronoun refers to will be frustrated.

J. _____ These connecting words—words like "however" and "finally"—provide the most formal kind of linkage.

K. _____ There are four types of these connectors: the connecting word, the pronoun, the repeated word and the synonym.

L. _____ When you write—and particularly when you revise—think about possible synonyms, but also about the other three connecting devices—and their pitfalls.

Order of the sentences: E-l, K-2, F-3, J-4, A-5, D-6, I-7, C-8, H-9, G-10, B-ll, L-12

Review the sentences and identify the connections that made it possible for you to find the correct order.

Now write a paragraph of between five and twelve sentences. (Instead of types of connections, try types of greetings, athletic shoes, weddings, whatever you know about.) Pay attention to making connections. Then write the sentences out one at a time. Cut them out, jumble them and give your paragraph to someone else to reassemble.

If that person can put the paragraph back together, you have probably written a connected paragraph.

3. Signal a Change in Direction

As you are revising a piece of writing, imagine that you are driving this prose as if it were a car. In the car behind, perhaps following too closely for comfort, is your reader. While you are tooling along, you are remembering that if you change lanes, make a turn, or stop and back up, you had better alert the driver-reader who is coming up fast in your rear view mirror.

Think of transitional links in writing as if they were hand signals to warn the reader that something is up. Below are some more-or-less generic transitional links. Pick a specific topic and write some sentences which could precede and follow some of these transitions. First, here's an example.

Transition: Yet behind the apparent fun is a serious purpose.

Example: Duck Soup *showcases the usual Marx Brothers absurdities. Groucho as Rufus T. Firefly, exalted leader of the comic opera nation of Freedonia, celebrates his inauguration with a silly Spanish dance. Harpo hears a bell ring and, as the ringing continues, dives toward a desk, answering one phone then another, finally grinning as he pulls a large alarm clock from his pocket. The military encounter between Freedonia and Sylvania transforms into a food fight.*

Yet behind the apparent fun is a serious purpose. *The film ridicules the political posturing, the jingoism, the treachery, and the shifting alliances that lead to modern wars fought with far more deadly weapons than tomatoes.*

Now compose a couple of paragraphs which one of the following transitions might link:

1. Yet, behind this apparent fun is a serious purpose.
2. Even though these early unsuccessful efforts were frustrating, they were a necessary proving ground for the triumphs which were to follow.
3. That's the official story, but these claims have little to do with the less pretty reality.
4. As a result of these unreasonable restrictions, the rebellion which followed seemed inevitable.

PART V: WRITERS CREATE CHOICES

- **Setting Your Prose in Concretes:**
  Thirteen Ways to Make the Most of Specifics

- **By the Same Token:**
  Two Ways to Make an Effective Comparison

- **Why Apples Aren't Oranges:**
  Seven Ways to Put Contrasts to Work

- **Way-Back-When Revisited:**
  Four Ways to Use the Past

- **Pilot Training for a Flight of Fancy:**
  Five Ways to Use Your Imagination

- **More than Just a Complete Thought:**
  Nine Ways to Write Classier Sentences

SETTING YOUR PROSE IN CONCRETES:
THIRTEEN WAYS TO MAKE THE MOST OF SPECIFICS

Essay

Arresting Specifics: Breaking the What-Ja-Ma-Call-It Habit

L ONG before "teacher renewal" became a minor industry, I developed my own program to keep my brain from dissolving into cafeteria creamed tuna. It went like this: every few months, I would try something definitely—even defiantly—not in the curriculum guide. That's how I came to orchestrate a wild and rejuvenating activity relevant to the topic of this section—the power of specifics.

The situation evolved when three refugees from the drama department presented themselves in my 7:30 A.M. expository writing class. While the very concept of 7:30 A.M. did violence to their artistic temperaments, they had no choice but to submit to this ordeal if they wanted to get to play rehearsal during the last period of the day. For myself, I knew from past experience that three drama students in one class was actor overload. I am no Lee Strasberg, but I did have an idea to make use of their talents and to buy myself a little peace. I put them to work carrying out a scheme I had been planning for some time. I wanted to see what the class could find out about communication if we sent these fearless exhibitionists out to place the following order at three different fast food restaurants: "I'd like some hot food, a drink, and dessert."

The three agreed that regardless of what was said to them they would go no further than to repeat this order. They'd leave if and when things began to get hairy and report back to us what happened.

I do not remember the specifics of each exchange, though I do recall how one canny counter person wiped out a good chunk of the budget I had set aside for this experiment by serving up a Double Whopper with cheese, Giant apple turnover, and a Jumbo Dr. Pepper. But it was a cranky Taco Bell manager who left us with something to remember. After some patient efforts to coax a more exact order from our man, the manager grew exasperated and said, according to the drama students, "If you can't be more specific, I will have to call the police."

Whether or not these were the fellow's exact words, back in class I pulled the lesson together. "See," I said, "vagueness can lead to big trouble." Now, many years later, I like to think that students from that class, about to label an object a thingamajig, doohicky, or whoosis will be confronted by a not-so-still, not-so-small voice intoning "If you can't be more specific, I am going to have to call the police."

1. Think Specifically

Writers with style never just eat breakfast. They munch on granola, wolf down hotcakes, savor Frosted Flakes, or gorge on jelly doughnuts.

You should not settle for the general. Keep asking yourself, "Like what?" "What else?" "What about it?"

In this way a statement like, "Every September I get the urge to buy school supplies" can become:

> *Every year about this time I get the urge to buy a copybook. And some of those little rectangular pink erasers that look good enough to eat. And a whole lot of those round reinforcements, which were supposed to be pasted around the holes in your loose-leaf paper but were more often made into designs on the inside cover of your loose leaf binder.*
> —Anna Quindlen

Use this model to try an "I get the urge" paragraph as you recall images set off by:

- Saturday or Sunday morning
- the first day of spring
- the Christmas season
- the Fourth of July
- an old song
- a particular photograph
- the first snow
- a trip to a former hometown

2. Pile Up Specific Examples

In any piece of writing, be generous with specifics. Too many specifics in a draft of a piece of writing is not like too much saffron in a paella. Specifics you can always take out, and large numbers of details make a rich prose stew.

The writer of paragraph "B" below, who comments on "trash" TV, could have settled for the minimum, something like "A."

A. *So far as I can tell, nothing of human capability has been excluded. The show is for those who wish to admit to or watch others admit to inadequacies ranging from a compulsive need to overspend on their credit cards to a hatred of their mothers.*

Instead she piles on the specifics:

B. *So far as I can tell, nothing of human capability has so far been considered too private, too serious, too silly, too gross, or too tacky to be exempted. ... There is nothing anyone can do; no misery, shame, folly, secret, guilt, dream, intimacy, crime, good turn, triumph, fatal error which might be framed by human lips that is not confessed to in ringing tones. Have you been fat, raped, sent to a reformatory, overspent on credit cards, committed adultery, killed someone with you motor car, been hooked on an illegal substance, hated your mother, betrayed your race, beaten your spouse's child, bought a baby, changed your sex, fallen victim to Alzheimer's disease, fathered your daughter's child? Topics such as these are daily fare on these programs.*
   —Adapted from *Punch* Magazine

Here's a game to pile up specifics in support of an idea: The A to Z List. First, state the idea. For instance: Anyone can put out a tabloid who knows how to sprinkle bizarre revelation with a mix of crime, celebrity, sex, addiction, disaster, disease, diets, pets, and kids—plus a dose of the paranormal and extraterrestrial.

Then produce A to Z examples, real or imagined:

Ape Marries New York Socialite

Bon-bons Can Help You Lose Weight

Cavemen Discovered Living in Wyoming

Dolly Parton Arranged John Lennon's Death

Elephants Stampede in Detroit, 20,000 Killed

Farrah Fawcett Battles Cocaine and Sean Penn

Ghost of Edgar Allen Poe Haunts Cleveland Antique Shop

Hidden Treasure Found in Shopping Mall

"**I** Ate My Children," Confesses California Housewife

Juggling Causes Cancer

Kentucky Truck Driver Becomes Werewolf

Liza Minelli Is Actually a Robot

Modern Technology Scares Away Aliens, Experts Claim

Nigerian Wombat Eats Royal Family

Occult Worshippers Hold Conference

People with Straight Teeth Report Happier Lives

Quit Smoking Through Underwater Therapy

Rap Star Fires Sensitivity Trainer

Sibling Rivalry Reported Low by Only Children

TV Radiation Can Cause Baldness

UFOs Kidnap Entire City of Detroit

Violence Can Lead to Death, Experts Report

Water Is Actually Phlegm of Aliens

X-Rays Aid Weight Loss

Y Chromosome Proclaimed Hoax

Zookeeper Releases Tiger in Civil Protest

    —Daniel Handler, age seventeen

Here are a few somewhat more serious list-generating ideas:

- The cacophony of city sounds is both exhilarating and stressful. List the sounds.
- The average Christmas gift finds its way to a garage sale or a Goodwill donation bag. List the gifts.
- Some jobs aren't worth doing for any amount of money. List the jobs.
- Possessions defined the Yuppies of the 1980s. List the possessions.
- On a first date, everything that can go wrong usually does go wrong. List the mishaps.

Try brainstorming an A to Z list with other people.

3. Choose Weighted Specifics

Remember, while you want your reader or listener to understand that you are a fair and reasonable person, your prose should not sound like an autopsy report. Biased specifics can animate your opinions.

Rather than: *San Francisco Giants' Outfielder Kevin Mitchell has promised to be more responsible. But even if he backslides and doesn't meet all his commitments to the fans and the club, wouldn't you still rather have him in left field than some well-mannered player who can't hit?*

Try: *Mitchell promises never to be bad again, but even if he backslides and doesn't show up for the teriyaki chicken at the Moose Club Awards Banquet, wouldn't you rather have him in left field than a choirboy who opens doors for old ladies but bats .211?* —Lowell Cohn

Turn some of the following general statements into examples rich in specific and biased detail.

- Rude driving by both sexes is one more indication of decline in civility. It used to be males drove aggressively to prove their macho; now women drive with equal combativeness to demonstrate their liberation.

- If you need further proof that this is the age of the elevated amateur, you need look no further than to the success of certain garage bands, camcorder filmmakers, and performance artists.

- Little League baseball requires kids to take on some of the worst qualities of adults. They live out the entire season in a state of stress, blame their mistakes on everyone but themselves, and come to believe that winning is all that matters.

- The secret to success in making television commercials is finding the right images for the right audience. The purveyors of beer, perfume, and luxury cars each manipulate a separate set of symbols.

4. Exaggerate Specifics Sometimes

Exaggeration is a way of bringing humor to your writing and is one form of humor which can be learned.

Read these excerpts from Dave Barry's review of the year 1992 and provide an exaggerated specific for each blank. For instance, in blank (1) Barry wrote "17." Barry's choices follow the excerpts.

January
Bill Clinton, a virtual unknown on the national scene, despite the fact that he has been governor of Arkansas since he was ____(1) arrives in New Hampshire with a truck containing ___(2) separate eight-point policies and enough hair spray to____(3)

August 20
General Motors announces that, in an effort to cut costs, it will___(4)

November 3
Clinton wins and announces that he may not be able to fulfill all of his campaign promises IMMEDIATELY, but he does expect, within the first one hundred days, to ask Congress to declare_____(5)

Barry's Answers: (1) 17 (2) 957 (3) immobilize the Brazilian rain forest (4) stop making cars (5) National Reed Instruments Week [Understatement is a type of reverse exaggeration.]

With others, create some entries for a similar review of the current year.

Now try turning up the sound on your writing to create overstated specifics to make a general point.

Examples:

General point: People seem to think that even a minute alteration in their dress affects their appearance.

Exaggerated Specifics: *"How is it that different things put on the same body can make us look alternately like living hell or a movie star? Excuse me, but why should the slightest change of color or cut determine whether we feel fit to lunch with Dustin and Meryl or to submit ourselves to medical science as a gift pack of donor organs?"*—Joan Frank

General Point: When Americans make a purchase, they want a choice.

Exaggerated Specifics: *"We don't even like restaurants with set menus. The right to substitute a tossed green salad for French fries is enshrined in the Constitution."*—Jane Walmsley

Create overstated specifics to make some of the following points:

- The "Elvis Lives" craze is going too far.
- Rooting for certain sports teams is a form of masochism.
- Grace under pressure is the character trait most needed to answer a personal ad.
- Opposites attract.
- A President of the United States is too isolated from everyday life to understand the needs of his constituents.
- Computer hackers live by their own rules.
- Advertisers of pet products know that many people treat their pets as humans.
- When it comes to judging art, some people equate high quality with weirdness and obtuseness.
- Teaching in many schools these days has very little to do with instructing students in reading, writing, and arithmetic.
- The commute hours provide a daily laboratory for the observation of man's baser instincts.

5. Define with Specifics

Dictionary definitions are general, but you can also define with specific examples. For instance, a pessimist, the dictionary says, is a person who expects the worst. Go further. How does a pessimist behave? What does she think when the boss merely grunts his morning recognition? What is her first thought when the phone rings in the middle of the night?

You can make particularly solid use of defining examples when you are exploring the meaning of words for which the dictionary gives little help. The dictionary defines "beautiful" and also "people." But "Beautiful People," as the term has been used since the 1970s, suggests a collection of attributes which Webster ignores. Here this subspecies is defined by examples of their behavior on the slopes of Aspen:

> Beautiful People are a breed distinct, like creatures from another planet.
>
> They turn their skis straight down the mountain at fifty miles an hour with a look of boredom on their bronze faces. The feet of the Beautiful People never hurt inside their boots.
>
> At the end of the day they immerse themselves in outdoor whirlpool baths heated to 160 degrees and afterward roll their long bodies in the snow.
>
> Then the Beautiful People go out to restaurants for elaborate and caloric meals which, because their metabolism is different from yours and mine, do not cause them to grow fat.
>
> Finally, they adjourn to the discotheques to dance the night away and form liaisons with Beautiful Persons of the other gender and awake in the morning in strange chalets, without hangovers and with their expressions of boredom intact.
>
> Unlike the rest of us, who would worry about such things as our toothbrushes, Beautiful People do not have morning breath.
>
> —C. W. Guswelle

In contrast to an orthodox dictionary definition, a definition by example may have an attitude.

Consider a subspecies you know a lot about. Define this type by example. Some suggestions:

- hacker
- hypocrite
- slacker
- feminist
- glutton
- showoff
- macho man
- perfectionist
- boor
- cynic
- bore
- hotdog
- optimist
- egotist
- wuss

6. Make Numbers Vivid

There's a reason insomniacs are advised to count sheep. It's not so much the sheep as the counting that puts them away. Unadorned numbers are an inexpensive soporific.

Statistics need to be made vivid, presented with style. Put your numbers into a specific context that gives meaning to the data.

Slice a Figure into Digestible Pieces: *Let's put the Chairman of the Board's "compensation" ($18,299,996) into perspective. That's $351,923 a week. That's $70,385 a day. That's $8,798 an hour. When the guy is caught at a thirty-second traffic light, his company wastes $73.32.* —Bill Mandel

Compare It with the Same Number in Other Contexts: *A billion seconds ago it was 1951. A billion minutes ago Jesus was alive and walking in Galilee. A billion hours ago no one walked on two feet on earth. And a billion dollars ago was 10.3 hours in Washington D.C. ...* —Alexander Trowbridge

Contrast It with Dramatically Different Numbers for the Same Phenomena: *Number of expert witnesses listed in the Lawyer's Desk Reference in 1970: 500. Today: 3,500.* —Harper's Index

Convert Numbers into Images: *If all the unemployed people in the U.S. were avocados, they would make a guacamole the size of Guam.* —Isadora Alman

Link Numbers to the Familiar: *The division of divorce is not the division of a cell that split into two equal parts, each happy and independent. If the total wealth of our marriage were represented by a pie like the kind that appears in magazines to show where your tax dollars go, her part of the pie would be national defense, my part would be Amtrak.* —Gary Powell

Contrast a Number with a Related Figure: *Amount the Reagan Administration budgeted for military bands in 1987: $154,200,000.*

Amount it budgeted for the National Endowment for the Arts: $144,900,000. —Harper's Index

Extrapolate Larger Numbers from Smaller Ones: *If you read every comic strip published in the* Washington Post, *as (former press secretary) Larry Speakes now claims President Reagan (did), it takes roughly eight minutes a day, which means by my tally, the (previous) leader of the free world spent a total of fourteen days, sixteen hours and forty-eight minutes of his presidency reading comics. Which explains a lot.* —Gary Trudeau

Take some numbers from your life worth noting or complaining about: your allowance or the wages on your job, the number of hours a week you spend on some unpleasant task, the number of times a day someone you know repeats an irritating phrase, the number of dates you've had in the past year.

Dramatize these numbers to make your attitude toward them clear.

7. Push for Pictures

A high school teacher gives his students the sentence, "Jones has the appearance of a college professor." He asks them to describe Jones. Of course, the teacher knows what the stereotypical college professor looks like: the salt and pepper beard, the Harris tweed coat, the baggy rumpled slacks and scuffed brown shoes, worn at the heels.

Then a student begins to read: "Jones is a short woman whose glasses dangle from a string around her neck…"

If you want your readers to watch the same mental movie you are watching, you'll need to make verbal pictures for them.

Try some specific, if stereotypical, versions of the following:

- a grunge fanatic
- a prosecuting attorney
- a science teacher
- an off-duty cop
- a politician

- a TV anchorman or woman
- an off-duty lifeguard
- a poet
- a Deadhead
- a librarian

Now describe someone you know who does not fit the stereotype he or she suggests by his or her occupation or special interest.

Close-ups: Helping Students See the Small Picture

I caution my students against Cast of Thousands Writing—that is, the essay that makes statements about humanity but shows us no individuals.

I use parts of videos which illustrate how the best of the epic film-makers have solved the problem of the broad brush. For example, during the exodus in the Cecil B. DeMille Biblical epic of the same name we see more than masses of people on the road. The camera cuts from scenes of sweltering humanity to close-ups of a dog, an old person, a lost, weeping child, a flock of geese, a mother giving birth in a wagon.

I then ask students to observe a large group and, as they write about their observations, move from long shots to close-ups.

Here is one student paragraph from a longer essay. It starts in long shot, moves in to close-up and then back to long shot:

> But there is a problem at Powell and Market—a lack of trust. In order to enter the Bank of America, one must insert an A.T.M. card into the slot on the side of the door! The tourist in polyester pants, carrying a Minolta 2FZ Special with wide-angle lens, grips it so tightly to her purse that her knuckles are white. Street people cast nervous glances at the police. The police do not trust the street people; the street people do not trust the police.
>
> —Laura Phillips, grade twelve

8. Choose Nouns over Adjectives

Nouns show; adjectives tell. Using nouns, you can present your attitude without insisting on your opinion.

Compare: *While angry demonstrators marched outside, demanding attention be paid to AIDS research, the homeless, and the economy, inside the Hilton Hotel ballroom President Bush addressed a fundraising luncheon for more than nine-hundred privileged **upper-class** business leaders and their guests, who were seemingly **unaffected** by the disruption outside.*

With: *While angry demonstrators marched outside, demanding attention be paid to AIDS research, the homeless, and the economy, inside the Hilton Hotel's ballroom, the President addressed a fundraiser at which more than nine-hundred business leaders and their guests dined on **poached salmon in dill sauce and cassava on a raspberry coulis.***

Write one-sentence descriptions of the rooms in which people with the following personality traits reside. Let objects and actions, not adjectives, convey the trait.

Example: The person is reclusive.
Description: *Oscar chooses a film from a week's supply of video rentals as the phone, unequipped with an answering machine, rings for the sixth time.*

Other Traits

▪ outdoorsy	▪ clean	▪ stuffy
▪ nostalgic	▪ sentimental	▪ ostentatious
▪ well-read	▪ flashy	▪ childish
▪ careless	▪ clumsy	▪ avant-garde

Can others identify the trait you are depicting?

9. Choose Specific Adjectives over General Ones

All adjectives are not equal. Choose those that are precise over those that are vague. "Inhibited," "inept," and "intelligent" have a specificity lacking in generalized adjectives like "boring," "superb," and "awesome."

A carefully chosen list of adjectives can define a character. A writer for the Style pages of the *Washington Post* describes Oliver North at the Iran-Contra hearings:

> *... a face that is fierce, furrowed, boyish, angry, lachrymose, goofy, sly, handsome, smug, indignant, dissembling, wounded, gap-toothed, peeved, resolute, naive, contemptuous, resentful, bright, wary, cocky, and five-o'clock shadowed.*

Find twenty precise adjectives to describe a public figure. Try your list on others. Do they know who you are talking about?

10. Choose Concrete Nouns over Abstract Nouns

Sometimes present a big idea as a specific and allow the reader to generalize.

The classical economist Adam Smith could have said: *It is the economic self-interest of others, not their good-heartedness, that assures us we will get the products we need.*

Instead he chose the less abstract, more specific: *It is not from the benevolence of the butcher, the brewer, or the baker that we expect our dinner, but from their regard to their own interest.*

Other Examples:

Not: (at the beginning of World War I) *It will be a long time before Europe recovers from this tragedy.*

But: *The lamps are going out all over Europe. We shall not see them lit again in our time.* —Sir Edward Grey, British foreign secretary

Not: *Violence against property can make an effective political statement.*

But: *The argument of the broken pane of glass is the most valuable argument in modern politics.* —Emmeline Pankhurst, British suffragette, 1912

Not: *Millions who are bored with life still long for immortality.*

But: *Millions long for immortality who do not know what to do with themselves on a rainy afternoon.* —Susan Ertz

Try expressing some of the following proverbial observations with more specificity:

Example: *Lost time is never found again.* —Folk saying
Can become: *Hours spent with "Gilligan's Island" reruns cannot be replayed in prime time.*

- Ability is of little account without opportunity.
- Fortune favors the audacious.
- Giving is better than receiving.
- Behind bad luck comes good luck.
- Better a bad excuse than none at all.
- Imitation is the sincerest form of flattery.
- Prosperity makes friends; adversity tries them.
- Brevity is the soul of wit.
- Out of sight, out of mind.

11. Choose Specific, Action-Filled Verbs

Find substitutes for the all-purpose verbs lazy writers love.

Particularly when you revise your writing, seek out action alternatives for some of the following basic, all-purpose verbs:

> *to be (in all its forms), to need, to come, to let, to have, to make, to know, to give, to take, to get, to say, to go, to show, to tell, to look, to see, to talk, to do, to want, to bring, to put, to see, to let.*

Here are four pairs of sentences detailing a writer's absent-mindedness. The first in each pair uses all-purpose verbs, the second uses more specific and less-often used verbs.

- I go through my handbag *looking* for the note I have *put* on the back of an envelope.
- I *ransack* my handbag, *poking* about for the note I'd *scribbled* on the back of an envelope.

- I *look* at "Good Morning America," hypnotized, when I should *be* in line at the bus stop.
- I *gape* at "Good Morning, America," hypnotized, when I should be *queued* up waiting for the bus.

- I *use* a large numbers of "Sorry I forgot your birthday" cards.
- I *devour* large numbers of "Sorry I forgot your birthday" cards.

- I *get* up and *go* to work on the 4th of July.
- I *hop* out of bed and *scramble* off to work on the 4th of July.

Focus on one of your traits. Write five sentences illustrating some specific behaviors associated with this trait. Revise the sentences, working for energetic, specific verbs.

Comment

Here's a somewhat less demanding variation on this challenge. Ask students to write pairs of sentences beginning with "I like ... " followed by an all-purpose verb in its infinitive form, and then try one with a lively verb.

Examples:

- I like to put peanut butter and jelly on whole wheat bread to make a sandwich.
- I like to slather peanut butter and jelly on whole wheat bread to create a sandwich.

- I like to take my bicycle through heavy traffic, going between the lines of immobile cars.
- I like to bicycle through heavy traffic, snaking through the lines of immobile cars.

Essay

Writing Conference

Student: *I don't understand what's wrong with these sentences.*

Me: *Which?*

Student: *These: "On our last camping trip it rained three days. We just stayed in our tent and utilized our food."*

Me: *You threw your food?*

Student: *Of course not. We ate it.*

Me: *See the problem. A lot of "ize" words—scrutinize, utilize—lack energy and precision. Would you say, "I utilize my tooth brush"?*

Student: *Not after what you just said.*

Me: *What would you say?*

Student: *I use my tooth brush.*

Me: *But what do you use it for?*

Student: *To brush my teeth.*

Me: *So why not, "I brush my teeth"?*

Student: *Then how do they know I used a toothbrush?*

Me: *Sometimes you've just got to trust your reader.*

Student: *Yeah. Well, my dad is always saying things like, "We are going to finalize the deal," and he's pretty successful.*

Me: *What could he say?*

Student: *Maybe he could say, "We are going to complete the deal," but he doesn't.*

Me: *Would he ask you if you had finalized your homework?*

Student: *No. He's not that kind of dad. He doesn't bug me.*

12. Discard Adverbs; Find Verbs

When you revise, look at your adverbs to make sure you need them. Don't settle for a flat verb jacked up by an adverb while you pass over a powerful specific verb that could do the job all by itself.

> **Instead of:** *Whenever I get a few extra dollars, I* **spend** *money* **recklessly***.*
> **Try:** *Whenever I get a few extra dollars, I* **splurge***.*

Try rewriting the following sentences, substituting a lively verb for the verb-adverb combination.

1. I *sat precariously* on the edge of my chair waiting for the announcement.
2. I *worried obsessively* about the details of the party.
3. The calculus problem *completely confused* me.
4. The speech went on and on, as I *moved about nervously* in my seat.
5. Before the prom, she *suddenly broke up with* her boyfriend.
6. Avoid him in the morning, as he *complains sourly* about everything.
7. I *grow silently angry* every time I hear his name.
8. He *secretly changed* the test results to improve his score.
9. He *ostentatiously disobeyed* the law.

Possible Answers: (1) perched, (2) fretted, (3) bewildered, (4) fidgeted, (5) dumped, (6) grumbles, (7) seethe, (8) doctored, (9) flouted

13. Try Out Alternative Verbs

Try out different verbs until you get the right one for your purpose. One way to develop this habit is to think of the alternatives to "he said." Work for precision. "'Shut up,' he explained,"* won't do. Here's some practice in choosing among alternative "said" verbs. Look over the list of verbs below, then write some dialogues of at least two sentences, but not more than four, each of which uses the word "pizza."

The Verbs

acknowledged	admonished	added	advised
allowed	barked	babbled	begged
blathered	blurted	cajoled	cautioned
complained	conceded	confessed	confided
demanded	demurred	dithered	droned
emphasized	gasped	gibbered	groaned
howled	insisted	instructed	interceded
interrupted	intoned	jabbered	jeered
joked	lied	maintained	managed
moaned	mumbled	muttered	objected
offered	ordered	parroted	piped
pleaded	pronounced	protested	purred
quipped	reasoned	remonstrated	reported
schmoozed	retorted	scoffed	screamed
scolded	shouted	shrieked	simpered
snapped	sniggered	sobbed	spluttered
spoke up	stammered	stressed	stuttered
swore	taunted	teased	ventured
wailed	warned	whimpered	whooped
	yammered	yelled	

*from Ring Lardner

Examples:

"Ma'am, I want a glass of ice water with a straw and a twist of lemon!" demanded the woman.

"Of course, for you, anything," muttered the waitress.

"Oh, ma'am. There's a fly on my pizza," the woman yammered.

"Shall I swat it away for you?" snapped the tired waitress, about to lose it.

—Danielle Wong, age seventeen

"You're nothing but a low-down, pizza-hogging, beer-guzzling couch potato," barked Thelma.

"Zwalup," Harry muttered unintelligibly, his eyes glued to the TV, as he rose to scream, "He's all talk and no action. Strike him out."

—Junna Ro, age seventeen

"Bark! Bark!" barked the dog.

"Purr … Purr … " purred the cat.

"They want some of our pizza," reasoned Stella.

"Don't be stupid!" scoffed Bill.

—Lesley Aiken, age seventeen

By the Same Token:
Two Ways to Make an Effective Comparison

1. Make Sure the Likenesses Eclipse the Differences

You can make a point by making a comparison, showing the way one thing is like another. Make sure, however, that you call attention to important, not irrelevant, similarities. Yes, a mouse and elephant are both grey, but that's about it.

Among the following comparisons, find some in which the differences overwhelm the similarities. Detail the differences.

- An oil executive on the subject of spills from oil tankers: *There are natural seeps all over this country. Oil in the water is a phenomena that has gone on for eons.*

- *My dad once told me that if I wanted to eat meat then I should be willing to watch the animal being slaughtered. I decided then and there I would rather give up hamburgers then watch Old Bessie get the ax. By the same token, if you support capital punishment, you should be willing to watch a televised execution.*
  —Letter to the Editor, *San Francisco Chronicle*

- *Just imagine if a teacher, in a unit on alcohol, was to describe in full detail the methods of getting drunk, or spend some time talking about drunk driving without offering any moral judgments as to whether driving while intoxicated was right or wrong, but say, "If you decide to drive and drink, here are some ways to avoid detection: this one is eighty-five percent safe, this one is ninety-two percent." We would think that teacher incompetent. In some sex education classes, this is what we are doing.*
  —Tottie Ellis

- A defense of the survivors of an airplane crash who resorted to cannibalism: *You cannot condemn what they did when it was the only possibility of survival. … Eating someone who has died in order to survive is incorporating their substance and it is quite possible to compare this with an organ transplant. Flesh survives when assimilated by someone in extreme need, just as it does when an eye or heart of a dead person is grafted onto a living person.*
  —Andres Rubiano, Bishop of Montevideo

- *There is no reason why a joke should not be appreciated more than once. Imagine how little good music there would be if, for example, a conductor refused to play Beethoven's Fifth Symphony on the grounds that his audience might have heard it before.*
  —A. P. Herbert

- McDonald's founder Ray Kroc responding to a question about the health value of McDonald's food: *Look, my friend, if you fix yourself a dinner of cake and ice cream, what are you going to do, blame Safeway for selling it to you? If you order a Coke or a milkshake at MacDonald's instead of a glass of milk or orange juice, whose fault is that?*

- Ted Turner defends the "colorizing" of the classic films he owns: *In the old days, no one griped that most of the movies were being shot in color and they were being seen on black and white television sets.*

- *It is not true that teaching teenagers how to use condoms encourages them to have sex. We teach them to use seatbelts. This does not encourage them to have collisions.*

- *If Wayne Gretsky is such a great hockey player, why can't he sing grand opera? If the Rolls-Royce is such a great car, why can't it cure the common cold? If those questions sound strange, try these:*

If we can spend billions of dollars on weapons of mass destruction, why can't we invest more in the education of our children? If we can help feed the Russians, why can't we find a cure for AIDS?
— Thomas Sowell (Sowell says that both sets of questions share the same form, and these questions are equally ridiculous.)

- A poster distributed in Minneapolis displays team pennants for the Pittsburgh Negroes, Kansas City Jews, San Diego Caucasians, and Cleveland Indians. The poster is captioned: *Maybe now you know how Native Americans feel.*

Write a letter to the editor in which you dispute the logic of one of these comparisons by calling attention to differences which overwhelm the similarities.

2. Link the Unfamiliar to the Familiar

You can describe an experience unfamiliar to a reader by comparing it to a more common one.

You do something others don't do:

How hard is hitting a baseball thrown by a big league pitcher? You ever walk into a totally black room full of furniture that you've never been in before and try to walk through it without bumping into anything? Well, it's harder than that.
  —Ex-Major Leaguer Ted Kluszewski

Or you see something others may have missed:

The televangelist is on TV, his wife at his side, as he pleads tearfully for pardon for his infidelities: *Staring at him, she finally nodded when he begged her for forgiveness. No radiant smile of pardon, even a drawn one of shared pain, accompanied the nod. Rather it was the nod a parent gives a child who has just delivered a well-rehearsed thank you to Grandma and Grandpa. Good boy.*
  —Stephanie Salter

Think of an unusual experience you have had or something unusual you have seen. Focus on one aspect of this experience; make a comparison connecting your special knowledge with what most everybody knows.

Comment

I've turned this challenge into an appropriate class activity during the weeks after epidemic senioritis debilitates large numbers of soon-to-be graduates. I ask students to write to sophomores and juniors, explaining senior experiences by, in part, comparing them with experiences with which not-yet-seniors may be familiar:

- *And then there's all the promotional video tapes they send from the colleges. Watching a string of these in a row is a lot like feeling compelled to sit through a blitz of 3 A.M. infomercials because you think you might miss something important.*

- *Remember when you were thirteen and wrote a love letter to Duran Duran? All day you'd be thinking about what the mail might bring and you'd run home from school looking for an answer that never came. Well, that's the way it is with college applications. Only eventually the colleges write back. And you may wish they hadn't.*

- *If, on a rainy day when you were six, you ever sneaked into your mother's closet and put on her heels and party dress, you know what it is like turning yourself out for the senior prom.*

Why Apples Aren't Oranges:
Seven Ways to Put Contrasts to Work

1. Contrast Likenesses

A successful contrast finds distinctions between similarities. Here a writer contrasts the new "cat America" with the disappearing "dog America."

> *Consider an America congenial to the dog: It was a place of nuclear or extended families, of someone always home, of children (or pets) looked after during the day by a parent (or owner), of open spaces and family farms, of sticks and leftovers, of expansiveness and looking forward to being outside; it was the America of Willa Cather and Lassie and Leon Leonwood Bean.*
>
> *Consider an America conducive to the cat: It is a place of working men and women without much time, of crowded cities, of apartment buildings with restrictive clauses, of daycare and take-out food, of self absorption and modest horizons; it is the America of Tama Janowitz and Blade Runner and The Sharper Image catalogue.*
> —Cullen Murphy

Use this model to write two paragraphs of contrast. Some possible topics: two periods of popular music, the politics of two decades, the difference between elementary school and high school or high school and college, two different eras in a business, a church, a city, a neighborhood. Decide which of the two you prefer and direct your details to support this view.

2. Juxtapose Contrasting Images

Writers of contrasts may need to find a place in the same sentence for a Miller Lite and a 1971 Bordeaux. Some ideas inspire a rich vein of contrasting specifics:

> *It is fair to say that* America's Funniest Home Videos' *popularity comes from its image of America. Not the America of Dan Rather, edgy and anxious, but of Bob Saget, goofy and well-meaning; not the America of crack dens, but of grandpa playing the harmonica with his nose; not the America of child abuse, but of kids drinking from the doggie bowl. Not the America of the have-nots, but of the have camcorders.*
> —Ellen Goodman

> *We have all been rendered shockproof. We have gone from The Platters to Snoopy Dog Dog, from Doris Day to Madonna, from the chaperone to the pill, from storks and cabbage patches to surrogate mothers and test-tube fathers, from the once unmentionable topic of homosexuality to gay rights.*
> —Nardi Reeder Campion

Extend the paragraphs above by providing contrasting examples of your own. Notice that each pair shares a commonality as well as a difference. Doris Day and Madonna are both blonde female singers, the chaperone and the pill both "birth control devices."

Now try your own paragraph of "not ... but" or "from ... to" contrasts.

Some possible topics:

> (A) the influence of money in modern sports, (B) the family, (C) the values of small-town life, (D) the behavior of celebrities, (E) medical practice, (F) manners and public behavior, (G) the role of women, (H) dating in the era of safe sex, (I) technology which replaces service employees, (J) fast food

The Evolution of a Writing Workout: Using Pictures to Contrast Now and Then

IT is the eighth inning of a Giants-Dodgers game. The guy in back of me has been screaming at the slumping Giant, Jack Clark, "Clark, you weenie" each time the slugger has come to bat. The guy is about 5'7" and 210 pounds. The flesh of his belly protrudes from under his Grateful Dead shirt and over his green paisley shorts. He is wearing a woo-woo cap, drinking beer, and burping. This time as Clark again approaches the plate, I am ready for another loud-mouthed tirade. What I am not ready for is the guy's Budweiser down my back. An hour and a half later, I am still smelling like a Sixth Street dive at closing time. I shrug it off: that's the sporting life.

A few days later I am looking through a book of historic baseball photos. Willie Mays is making the catch of Vic Wertz's fly ball in the 1954 World Series. But what I am noticing is the fans. Overwhelmingly male, they sit erect. They wear neat, clean sport shirts. Some are even wearing suits.

I start thinking of what can be learned by contrasting the same types of photographs from different eras. That's when I devise the Yearbook Project. From the school archives, students dig out yearbooks back to the 1940s. They write about their observations:

- *In 1941, every seventeen-year-old male graduate had the rigid, serious, adult look one might associate today with an uptight married man of twenty-five.*
- *In 1960, no girls wore pants in the group photos; in 1967, a smattering; by the 1980s, at least half.*
- *1958. Three non-white faces in one group photo. A first.*

I begin to think of other "then and now" possibilities for students. They can use photographs of neighborhoods, school dances, and, depressing as their conclusions might be, baseball games.

3. Spotlight Opposites

The strongest contrasts face off opposites.

She was as *affable* as her boyfriend was *abrasive*.
Not: She was as *affable* as her boyfriend was *sloppy*.

One may be both affable and sloppy. It is unlikely that a person would be both affable and abrasive. These words are close to opposites.

Below are some adjectives that can be used to describe personality and behavior, useful words you may not use often. Find opposites for some of them. For instance, the opposite of "mercurial" could be "level-headed." Then consider two people who are linked in some way but have opposite personality qualities.

Try two anchors on a news show, two teachers of the same subject, a brother and sister, a president and vice-president. Apply to them a pair from your list of opposites, then write paragraphs to support your distinction.

- bawdy
- blasé
- enigmatic
- canny
- capricious
- caustic
- docile
- dour
- ebullient
- fastidious
- flamboyant
- frugal
- ghoulish
- pedantic
- gregarious
- haughty
- innocuous
- insipid
- irascible
- languid
- magnanimous
- malleable
- mercurial
- meticulous
- narcissistic
- nocturnal
- nomadic
- predatory
- profligate
- prosaic
- prudent
- quixotic
- reticent
- sanctimonious
- sophomoric
- taciturn
- venerable
- vindictive
- wry
- zealous

4. Make Distinctions

When we think about moral questions and public issues, we often make distinctions—that is, contrasts—between similar beliefs and behavior.

Here are several groups of present or proposed government restrictions on behavior. If you favor one but not others in the grouping, can you make a distinction between or among them? Write a paragraph contrasting the policies.

1. Require motorcycle riders to wear helmets.
    Require bicycle riders to wear helmets.
    Require drivers to wear seat belts.

2. Prosecute people for using marijuana.
    Prosecute people for selling marijuana.
    Prosecute people for using heroin and crack cocaine.
    Prosecute people for selling heroin and crack cocaine.

3. Ban or regulate pornography.
    Ban or regulate hate literature.

4. Restrict smoking in public places.
    Outlaw the wearing of fragrances at public meetings.

5. Arrest people for buying and selling sex.
    Restrict private sexual practices between consenting adults.

6. Draft people into the armed forces in time of national emergency.
    Draft all eighteen-year-olds to perform some form of national service.

7. Ban the death penalty.
    Ban abortions.

5. Make the Most of Contradictions

Have you seen photographs that catch someone who appears to have wandered onto the wrong set: a bouffanted and blue-haired society matron at a soup kitchen, serving up dainty portions of holiday cranberry sauce? Richard Nixon, in suit and tie, walking alone on a California beach? Writers, as well as photographers, find ironic contrasts between a setting and a person. This writer describes the environment and then the man:

> It is glorious outside, a twilight saturated with gold light on the University of California at Davis campus. Small insects dance like motes in the silky haze, and skylarking undergraduates shout their delight at being young and alive and away from the books. Frisbees fly and you can smell the smoke from the barbecue fires off campus, almost taste the beer being pounded down.
>
> But inside, here in this room in Freeborn Hall, the Doctor Doom of American belles-lettres sucks in carcinogenic gasses from the latest in the chain of Pall Malls smoked for fifty-two of sixty-six years, and spreads layers of gloom like one of those modern artists who use trowel instead of brush.
>
> The earth is not dying, Kurt Vonnegut is saying; it is dead.
> —Jerry Carroll, San Francisco Chronicle

Use this model to write about a person set off in sharp contrast to his or her environment. Some possible topics:

- a child in church
- a young, inexperienced teacher in a rowdy classroom
- a mother chaperoning her twelve-year-old daughter and the daughter's friends to a rock concert
- a homeless beggar on an exclusive shopping street
- a teenager on a prom date at a fancy restaurant.

Try for a situation you have, in fact, observed.

Comment

Here's a student paper that illustrates a variation on this workout. This observation does not describe the environment of the church, but it does, through its detail, present the tension between the kids and their environment.

Sunday Best

11:07—The children's choir wriggles and fusses during the first scripture reading. The boys and girls, ranging from seven to ten, anxiously await their moment of glory in front of the congregation when they will sing "We the Children." Several of the girls sit quietly with their hands folded in their laps. The boys, however, are busy balancing choir folders and hymnals on their heads, whispering loudly.

11:26—A little blonde-haired girl two pews in front of me turns around. She sees me looking her way and starts a game of peek-a-boo behind the pew. Every time her head bounces up and her eyes meet my smiling face, she giggles and grins, quickly ducking behind the pew again.

11:35—During the sermon, a boy of about four colors dinosaurs and spaceships with Crayolas. He is quite content sitting on the floor, using the pew as a desk. One of his crayons rolls off the pew and drops to the wooden floor. The sound resounds throughout the sanctuary. His mother bends down to pick up the crayon, putting her index finger to her lips, signaling her son to be quiet.

11:38—Several teenage girls to my left laugh to themselves, constantly "shushing" each other. Writing notes back and forth on the church bulletin, they tell each other last week's gossip.

11:54—Everyone stands in unison for the last hymn, except an expectant mother of twins to my right. She takes up much room in the pew, sprawled out, allowing her oversized belly to rest comfort-

ably. She caresses her stomach, smiling and glowing, then registers a startled wince: One more child is squirming in church.

12:13—Children of all ages swarm to the cookies and punch carefully laid out for them. One girl who can barely reach the top of the table accidentally knocks over a cup of juice. It's quickly cleaned up by an observant adult. Crumbs and spilt punch cover the table, the rug, and the fronts of the children's Sunday clothes.

—Laura Snyder, age seventeen

6. Accent What Isn't

Overheard conversation after a high society party: *You remember her. You were talking to her. She was the one without the face-lift.*

A person or situation can be defined by what it is not. Note the emphasis on the negative in the following:

> *I was a war baby. Born in 1944. Which means I am not a baby boomer and therefore do not count. Products are not designed, neighborhoods are not gentrified, and fish are not blackened for my benefit. Presidential candidates do not choose running mates with me in mind.* Time *magazine does not care what I think. And there's no television show called "Fortysomething."*
> —Linda Ellerbee

> *My reasons for running, unlike those of the vast majority of the nation's twenty million joggers, have nothing to do with toning my body or nurturing my cardiovascular system.*
>
> *I do not run to build self-confidence, reduce anxiety, overcome depression, combat insomnia, or enhance my creativity.*
>
> *I do not run in search of God, existential truth, nonstop fornication, Coleridgian highs or Wordsworthian intimations of immortality.*
>
> *I do not even run because it is my dream to be interviewed on the All-Sports Cable Channel.*
>
> *I run—to put it as straightforwardly as I can—so that I can eat more.*
> —Mike Vare

> On Fred Astaire: … *As the years went on, I found something else about him that I admired tremendously. It was that I knew very little about him. I didn't read about his love life or about him punching someone in a night club. I didn't read about him storm-*

ing off a set, feuding with a director, fighting with the press, or babbling about what he liked to eat, what he liked to drink, snort, or smoke. He did his work, went home, closed the door, and said, 'That's it, world. You get my performance. The rest belongs to me.'
    —Mike Royko

Try one of the following:

- Consider a person who behaves differently from others who do the same job. (Royko)
- Contrast the common motivations for pursuing an activity with your motivations. (Vare)
- Contrast your own status with that of the members of some group to which you don't belong (Ellerbee)

In each case, let the negatives do the work, as in the models.

7. Classify

There are three classes of people. Those who see. Those who see what they are shown. Those who do not see.
—Leonardo di Vinci

Here Leonardo is making a classification. A classification is another way to show how similar things are different. Start with the idea that most any noun can be divided into subcategories. Take "mail." When the mail arrives at your home, you start classifying in spite of yourself. Your mind pigeonholes the personal letters, the bills, the junk mail, the magazines—all different, but all mail.

Writers create classifications as a way of sharpening ideas. Three examples:

1.

Holding hands in a movie theater is supposed to be romantic … Romantic, indeed!… Hand holding is torture. The reason, of course, is that there are all kinds of girl hand-holders. Like these:

The Bone Surgeon—She is majoring in bone structure at college, and she uses your hand as a guinea pig. Her experiments are quite painful. She explores each one of your fingers, one at a time, and tugs them to make sure they are really attached to the rest of your hand. Beware of this girl. She leaves permanent damage.

The Hair Patter—The girl hand-holder in a movie that really irritates me is the one that pats her hair and doesn't let loose of your hand. You are in the best part of the movie when all of a sudden you find your hand patting the top of her head.
—Dan Valentine

(Other types in this classification: The Nail Chewer, The Pincher, The Ring Presser, The Ripper, Miss Icy Fingers, The Wrestler, The Thumb Holder)

2.

One rough classification I have found useful is between what I call the pilots and the passengers. Some people, temperamentally and by training, seem to be pilots, and some seem to be passengers. And rarely do these two traits overlap.

The pilots have to direct their own pattern of behavior or they feel upset; the passengers have to be piloted or they feel insecure. Putting a pilot in a passenger's position can induce many nervous illnesses—for instance, I believe that carsickness on the part of a young child is a symptom of a pilot-type who is forced to become a passenger-type.

—Sydney Harris

3.

Of course, the meaning of a smile depends on the situation. A weak smile as one person attempts to squeeze past another in the theater after the play has begun says, "I'm sorry." A broad grin as someone scores the winning point in a tennis match says, "Gotcha!" A carefully cultivated smile at an attractive member of the opposite sex at a cocktail party says, "I'd like to get to know you better."

—Bernard Feder and Elaine Feder

Using the three selections above as inspiration, fill in the blanks in each of the following sentences. Choose one. Create the category and develop the specifics.

1. There are all kinds of _____. (hand-holders)
2. The world can be divided into _____ and _____. (pilots and passengers)
3. Different types of _____ have different meanings. (smiles)

Comment

Here are three out-of-whack classifications, two purposely skewed, one unintentionally off-balance. You can pull these out for students who need a special challenge. Can they explain their uneasiness with these categories?

The world is divided into two types of people. Those with six fingers and those without.
—Ned Rhomer

There are four kinds of people in the world: those in love, the ambitious, the observers, and the stupid. The most happy are the stupid.
—Hippolyte Taine

… (from) a certain Chinese encyclopedia entitled Celestial Emporium of Benevolent Knowledge. *On those remote pages it is written that animals are divided into (a) those that belong to the Emperor (b) embalmed ones (c) those that are trained (d) suckling pigs (e) mermaids (f) fabulous ones (g) stray dogs (h) those that are not included in this classification (i) those that tremble as if they were mad (j) innumerable ones (k) those drawn with a very fine camel's hair brush (l) others (m) those that have just broken a flower vase (n) those that resemble flies from a distance.*
—from Luis Borges, "The Analytical Language of John Wilkins"

Way-Back-When Revisited:
Four Ways to Use the Past

The more writers know about their heritage and the heritage of others, the better they will be able to make points about the present by referencing the past.

1. Manipulate Anachronisms

An anachronism mixes past and present sometimes accidentally, as in the case of the jumbo jet spotted flying through the frame of a western set in 1880, but sometimes purposefully, as in the following example:

> *Species have come and gone for millions of years, but now the Green Bigots want to bring this evolutionary process to a halt. Thank heaven there was no Sierra Club when the dinosaurs were around, or there wouldn't be any human beings today.*
> —Thomas Sowell

> *Thomas Jefferson might have had a very different idea about freedom of speech and religion if he had ever had to push himself through a band of airport Hari Krishnas while he was trying to make a connecting fight.*

> *Why is it that modern moralists are so squeamish about violence in the movies? They never seem to ask if the violence serves some purpose. If they had been around in Elizabethan England, they would have been campaigning to remove the eye-gouging scene from* King Lear.

> *If Shakespeare were writing* Henry IV *today, would he feel pressure to make the fat Falstaff a jogging vegetarian?*

Try making a point by thrusting a modern person or type into the past or bringing a historical figure into a modern situation.

2. Draw on a Shared Heritage

The joke goes: "Does the name Pavlov ring a bell?"

The reference here is to the Russian scientist Pavlov who conditioned dogs to salivate for food when they heard a bell. If you got the joke, it's because you understand the allusion. An allusion is an implied reference to a historic event or person—as in this case—or to a work of literature, music, art, or popular culture.

You can help make your point by alluding to people, events, stories, and familiar sayings to which—you hope—your reader can connect. Of course, there is no guarantee that a specific reader will have the slightest idea what you are talking about. Sometimes this ignorance doesn't matter. People will take a stab at figuring out allusions from context. But keep your audience in mind. Too many flights into obscurity and readers will get up and leave.

The following statements were all directed to a general audience. Can you explain the allusion each contains? If you don't understand the specific reference, how much can you figure out from context?

- *Half reporter/half showman, Geraldo Rivera is equal parts D'Artagnan, Crusader Rabbit, Horatio Alger and P. T. Barnum.*
  —Cynthia Robbins, *San Francisco Examiner*

- *If Frank Sinatra and Nancy Reagan ever got beyond exchanging confidences, swapping Hollywood gossip, and reminiscing about the good old days, then it surely is the most remarkable coupling since Leda and the Swan.*
  —Liz Smith

- Former French President François Mitterrand on Margaret Thatcher: *She has the eyes of Caligula and the mouth of Marilyn Monroe.*

- Ray Gandolf on Muhammad Ali at thirty-nine: *He floats like an anchor, stings like a moth.*

- *We are born princes and the civilizing process makes us frogs.*
  —Eric Berne

- Boxing writer A. J. Libeling on the style of former middle-weight champion Gene Fulmer: *At times, before throwing a punch he pulls his right elbow back behind his ear, as if drawing a longbow at Crecy.*

- *While standing in the shower the other day, fully dressed, sponge in hand, I thought to myself, what am I doing here? If stall showers had existed back in the days of ancient Greece, Sisyphus would have been doomed to spend his eternity trying to get the grout between the tiles clean (and they didn't even have Comet).*
  —John Stark, *San Francisco Examiner*

- *The lament for vanished standards is an old art form: Besieged gentility cringes, indignant and vulnerable, full of memories, before a present that behaves like Stanley Kowalski: crude, loud, upstart, and stupid as a fist.*
  —Lance Morrow, *Time*

- Judith Martin (Miss Manners) on 1960s "do-your-own-thing" behavior: *This is what I call the Jean-Jacques Rousseau School of Etiquette. The problem being that in our natural state we're not all that likable.*

Allusions often call on persons from history, literature, and popular culture to represent qualities. Think of persons who could represent each of the following qualities:

- blind ambition
- false humility
- physical strength
- excessive pride
- uncompromising stubbornness

- unwavering faith in a cause
- naive gullibility
- compulsive neatness
- unchecked gluttony
- consistent good humor

Express this connection in a sentence or two.

Example: *Physical strength*—Each morning Jerry, the Hercules of 46th Street, left home for his construction job, brimming with energy. Each evening he returned, wiped out after too many labors.

3. Try for Fresh Allusions

Push yourself beyond Pandora's box and Achilles' heel to less predictable allusions. Practice with the following list, incorporating some of the allusions with which you are familiar into appropriate sentences. Remember, your job is not to define or explain the term, but to transport it to another appropriate context.

Example: *Robin Hood*—Luxury taxes, graduated income taxes, and other Robin Hood schemes that claim to promote the general welfare at the expense of the rich, in reality, interfere with a free market and diminish opportunity for all groups.

- Alice in Wonderland
- David vs. Goliath
- Archie Bunker
- Charles Addams
- 1984
- Clint Eastwood
- Godot
- K-Mart
- The Marlboro Man
- Mr. Rogers
- Charlie Brown
- Steven Spielberg
- Willy Loman
- Dennis the Menace
- Gloria Steinem
- The Titanic
- Barbie
- Buck Rogers
- Holden Caulfield
- Disneyland
- Edsel
- Mark Fuhrman
- Hugh Hefner
- Mother Theresa
- Ralph Nadar
- Rambo
- Joseph McCarthy
- Walter Mitty
- Jay Gatsby

4. Make a Point with Classic Stories

Familiar and not-so-familiar tales can advance your argument.
Christopher Hitchens on political correctness:

> *You remember the end of* Peter Pan? *When the little light that
> represents Tinkerbell is growing dim and the children in the audience
> are told if they don't clap and keep clapping Tinkerbell will die? Well,
> that's how Washington feels right now. If you don't go along, you get
> looked at as though you've just shot Tinkerbell in the face.*

What contemporary points can be derived from each of the following tales?

- The robber Procrustes, in Greek legend, placed all who fell
  into his hands upon an iron bed. If they were longer than the
  bed, he cut off the over-hanging parts; if they were shorter, he
  stretched them until they fit.

- An ugly woman saw a beautiful woman frowning and beating
  her breasts. She said, "Now I know how to become beautiful," so she frowned and beat her breasts. The people of the
  village locked themselves in their houses.
  —Taoist Parable

- In ancient Greece, a man wanted to sell a distant house. He
  carried around a brick from the house as a specimen to show
  potential buyers.

- A scene from *Monty Python and the Holy Grail:* King Arthur
  and his knights come upon a belligerent knight who is not
  going to let them pass. The knight, covered from head to toe
  in armor, begins haranguing Arthur and his men as if he is
  backed by thousands.

Exasperated, Arthur finally acts, whacking off the man's arm.

"A flesh wound," scoffs the knight.

Arthur can't believe this. He starts hacking away at the knight: the other arm, a leg. More taunts. The other leg.

The pugnacious knight is finally reduced to a head and torso, twisting in the dirt, still hollering threats as Arthur and his men ride off.

- Al Capp's 1950s cartoon detective Fearless Fosdick, when assigned to protect the public from a can of poisoned baked beans that had been purchased from a grocery, barges into the house of anyone ready to sit down to a meal of baked beans and shoots that person dead, thus eliminating the possibility that his target would die from bean poisoning.

- A man loses his wallet and looks for it under a lamp post because that's the only place there is enough light to see.

- A young woman dressed in rags arrives one evening at a castle in the forest and asks to spend the night. The prince of the castle invites the young woman to sleep on a pile of soft mattresses. As he has placed a tiny pea under one mattress, the young woman awakens the next morning complaining of a sore back. The prince understands that anyone with such a heightened sensitivity is no ordinary young woman. He recognizes her as a true princess.

Recall a story, joke or anecdote that can be made to teach something about contemporary life. Tell the story. Connect it to the point about modern experience.

PILOT TRAINING FOR A FLIGHT OF FANCY:
FIVE WAYS TO USE YOUR IMAGINATION

How Many Points Off for Imagining?

I have stopped giving glib answers to honest questions. After three decades, I am admitting that my cleverness is no match for teenage earnestness.

I bring this up here because one of my stock flip responses relates to the connection between imagination and non-fiction writing, the subject of the workouts in this section.

I summon this bit of waggishness when, on the first day of expository writing class, a student asks, "Do we get to do any creative writing in here?"

I've learned to say, "All writing is creative writing."

About the twenty-eighth time I say this, however, something is different. I have one of those out-of-body experiences that has made me a better teacher. That is, I hear myself saying the words as if I were a student, listening. From my detached perspective, "All writing is creative writing" now sounds slick and dishonest, a slogan some ad person might run up the flag pole.

The twenty-ninth time the question comes up, I am ready. I say, "I'll take that question up tomorrow," and this time the postponement is not a way of saying, "Forget it." The next day we *do* consider creative writing in exposition, however obliquely. I pose this fanciful proposition, "We are beginning a campaign to make Groundhog Day a school holiday. Rather than just listing reasons why we think this reform is a good idea, we wish to present our case in ways that will get attention. What form could the argument take?" I add, "We aren't concerned here with specific arguments, but with the variety of writing forms—poems or television commercials, say—that might advance this cause."

I provide examples which make clear it's okay to fool around. I suggest the form could be a news story detailing the efforts of groundhog advocates to lobby the Board of Education or an imaginary interview with a ten-year-old groundhog owner in which she describes the critter's many virtues.

I suggest we brainstorm, but I am not getting much help. The idea is just too ridiculous; I am trying too hard. We are all embarrassed; even the grade-grubbers are squirming. But I can't quit now, or so I believe. I make a few more pathetic suggestions and finally bail out when I just happen to remember that students are going to need the rest of the period to share ideas for decorating their writing folders.

But this story has a happy ending. My performance, however absurd, pays off. Within a week one student has written an argument for the abolition of homework, taking the form of an imaginary report from a national education commission. Another student submits a slice of a courtroom drama in which the principal is on trial for forbidding girls to try out for football. I share these with the class, and we are suddenly caught in the middle of an epidemic of imagination run wild.

Moral: Don't count your teaching fiascos before they hatch.

1. Envision Change

If you have an idea to make things better, imagine a specific world with your plan in place. Suppose, for instance, you want to move the White House to the middle of the country, someplace like Omaha. What would be the effect of this change?

You imagine: The President could do a better job because he would have more of a chance to be a regular person. He could live on quiet tree-lined street in a big house with a lawn that he could cut. He could root for the high-school basketball team and drop down to the bingo game at the American Legion Hall on Saturday night where he would find out that the issues that dominate embassy receptions and "Face the Nation" are not always important to ordinary people.*

Consider a change you'd like to see. Imagine some of the specific results. Some possibilities:

- The countries of the world adopt an artificial language, such as Esperanto, as a single universal language.

- Your state is divided into two states.

- One of the Ten Commandments (choose which) in addition to "Thou shalt not kill" is made a law with penalties.

- A lifetime "ceremonial President" for the United States, one to cut ribbons and attend state funerals, is chosen by lot.

- Every neighborhood has a cop who walks a beat.

- Lawyers are disqualified from holding public office.

- A law is passed guaranteeing everyone six weeks vacation.

- Professional baseball and football teams are required by the league to hire only players who have grown up in the vicinity of the team's location.

- Local governments provide, at public expense, a bicycle for all people who stop driving their cars.

- People are allowed to designate how their tax money is spent.

- Dogs are banned from cities.

- Professional basketball teams are limited to rosters on which no more than one-third of the players are over six feet and none is over seven feet.

- Teachers are required to submit to regular psychological fitness exams administered by professionals.

- A national election is held for "Presidential Poet Laureate." Under a guarantee of immunity, she criticizes government policy as she wishes, like the fools in Shakespeare.

*Based on a suggestion by Bob Greene.

2. Create a Better World

Move beyond nitty-gritty, everyday unpleasantness. Imagine small utopias. The intersections of a city do not have to be full of drivers pushing beyond the crosswalks, stopping all movement, clogging nearby streets. Heartburn, obscenities, and fist fights need not be the by-products of city driving.

Change this world, not with sci-fi technology, but by imagining drivers who unfailingly stop at red lights, wait their turn, and smile at pedestrians and at each other.

Consider a job, a school, a class, a relationship, a family, or a church. Write about reality and the ideal. Fantasy can help make things happen.

3. Invent a *Before* and *After*

Imagine a context for the bits and pieces of lives you observe. The woman who lives across the street, the one who is never in a hurry, one day runs from her house, jumps in her car, slams the door violently, and pulls out, burning rubber. What happened? What is going to happen?

Try answering these questions when you spot something that is slightly or significantly out of the ordinary:

Suppose you notice for the first time one of those tiny man-made lakes along the freeway. A man is in a small rowboat, fishing. He is wearing an Eddie Bauer jacket and a baseball cap covered with lures and hooks and flies. The lake is packed with dozens of rowboats just like his.

You ask, what happened earlier?

Did he set the alarm for 4 A.M. and stock his ice chest with beer and sandwiches?

You ask, what will happen later?

Will he show off his catch to his wife and kids and invite the neighbors over for a fish feast grilled on a backyard Weber?

Be on the alert for the next observed moment that strikes you as special. Record the present. Imagine the before and after.

4. Imagine the Next Step

You can criticize an idea by taking the concept further.

A critic of Whittle Communications' Channel One, the program which has provided video equipment to schools in exchange for allowing Whittle's news to come into classrooms, complete with commercials, asks:

> *What next? Will we have Tylenol financing the school gym if administrators agree to pass out Tylenol each morning?*

Or another example:

> *I don't mind the question (of whether I've ever used drugs) but I'm afraid of what your next question will be: Do I live with my wife? How many times do I have sex with my wife? Do my dogs run around with dogs of the same gender? No, I've never smoked pot or taken any illegal drugs.*
> —Representative Joe Moakley, D-Mass.

But be careful not to go too far:

> *If it is true that fewer people are killed driving at fifty-five than at sixty-five, the proponents of reduced speed limits will want to save still more lives by lowering the speed limit to forty-five, then thirty-five, down to zero at which point no one would be killed because no one would be driving.*

If you disagree with any of the following policies, demonstrate your disapproval by extending the idea with less generally acceptable examples:

- Once the precedent of a ban on TV beer advertising is set, we have lots of other bad habits in need of control ...

- If we are going to have a National Football League rule that penalizes a team if its fans make excessive noise because such behavior creates a home-team advantage, what kind of rule changes can we expect next to limit this advantage?

- Now it's possible to get all kinds of information about a child in the womb. A male child, for instance, in a family with a history of hereditary diseases that affect only males, could be identified and aborted. But that's just for starters...

- If all an Equal Rights Amendment did was to guarantee equal employment rights for women, that would be one thing, but the concept opens the door for many other changes...

- Cities seem to see nothing wrong with inviting low-flying Blue Angels in to perform noisy and scary stunts over the town. If they are willing to expose us to this degree of danger and inconvenience for the sake of a show, what may we expect next?

Identify some existing or proposed policies with which you disagree. Critique them with examples that extend the concept.

5. Imagine the Future Based on the Past

Because much of life is "déjà vu all over again," you can use the past to imagine the future.

Look for the pattern in repetitious events.

According to this piece of office bulletin board folklore, workers know what's coming when a new idea surfaces at the firm:

The Six Stages of Production: (1) Wild Enthusiasm, (2) Total Confusion, (3) Utter Despair, (4) Search for the Guilty, (5) Persecution of the Innocent, (6) Promotion of the Incompetent.

More specifically, in 1992, a writer predicts the future of the tarnished royal Sarah "Fergie" Ferguson, based on what has happened to similar faded celebrities:

She'll settle in the United States. You can almost predict what will follow: A 'No Excuses' jeans ad, a string of tacky affairs (Donald Trump, Sylvester Stallone, Wayne Newton), more bad behavior in public, a stint at the Betty Ford Clinic, a People *magazine exclusive in which she details her sober new lifestyle, a cleansing tell-all memoir, a sportingly self-satirizing cameo in a 'Naked Gun' movie, and then marriage, to either George Hamilton or Joan Lunden's ex-husband. Finally, she earns the forgiveness of her adopted country persons, and for this Fergie is rewarded with the American equivalent of a tiara and a throne. She gets her own talk show.*
—Joan Millman, *San Francisco Examiner*

Based on what you have observed, can you identify stages of the following: a college or high-school course, a family vacation, the baseball season of a loved but untalented team, a marriage, an affair, a Saturday night party, the career of a rock group.

MORE THAN JUST A COMPLETE THOUGHT: NINE WAYS TO WRITE CLASSIER SENTENCES

Essay

The Simple Sentence

IS there a teachers' lunchroom in the U.S.A. where someone is not now expressing frustration over "the child who can't write a sentence?" This monologue begins by bemoaning the problems of the girl in fourth period, expands to the entire tenth grade, finally focusing on the source of the problem: Kids Today. Of course, this teacher has reason to be irritated, since writing a sentence is so easy.

You need only have an idea, making sure that this idea is expressed with a verb, which, rather than just lying empty and passive, allows its subject—preferably a concrete noun—to move someplace or feel something, agreeing all the while in person and number with its verb, which has not shifted tense or been loaded with unnecessary auxiliaries as it pushes forward the sentence that began by making a link to the previous sentence and now, by introducing new information, which, along with all other parts of the sentence, is clearly referenced, correctly modified and grammatically balanced, will end with a period, question mark or explanation point—but never with a preposition.

1. Build Sentences on a Subject-Verb Core

You will write sharper sentences if you think of yourself as a verbal shadow boxer, delivering one-two jabs, poking out clean, powerful subject-verb combinations. When your prose is connecting, you can almost hear the thwack as these sentence parts hit the page.

Today's scientists create fat-free pizza.

Not: A method has been developed which scientists use to make fat-free pizza.

We should start.

Not: We should not have any hesitation to get going.

Here is some practice at making and expanding a sentence with a powerful subject-verb core.

Step 1: Look over the lists of nouns and verbs which follow on pages 165 and 166. Then, using these lists, write four sentences, each with a subject, verb, and object. Choose a subject from each of the three columns of nouns and a fourth subject from any of the three columns. Then choose a verb from the list of verbs and an object from any of the three columns of nouns. You may make nouns and verbs plural, put the verbs in an appropriate tense, and add auxiliaries. You may also add articles (a, an, the) and possessive pronouns (his, her, our, their, my). The sentences should make sense.

Examples:
- Joggers prize karate.
- His Frisbee zapped a P.E. teacher.
- Poverty can squelch the American Dream.
- The weatherperson pooh-poohed the possibility.

Step 2: Add prepositional phrases and adjectives which clarify the basic clause.

His out-of-control Frisbee zapped the P. E. teacher *in the head.*
For many, poverty can squelch the American Dream.
The confident weatherperson pooh-poohed the possibility *of*
thunderstorms.

Step 3: Add appositives, which follow and rename nouns and give information about the subject or object.

Joggers prize karate, *a skill* which could save their lives.
The confident weatherperson, *a man more given to opinion than*
analysis, pooh-poohed the possibility of thunderstorms.

Step 4: Add clauses beginning with "who," "which," or "that."

Joggers *who run in isolated areas* prize karate, a skill which could
save their lives.

Step 5: Add clauses beginning with "after," "although," "because," "if,"
"until," "when," "while."

For many, *although they arrive in the U. S. with high hopes,* poverty can squelch the American dream.

Step 6: Add an "ing" participle phrase.

His out-of-control Frisbee, *taking on a life of its own,* zapped the
P. E. teacher in the head.

Nouns

Category 1—Living Things
Bart Simpson, celebrity, body builder, rapper, quarterback, referee, Yuppie, waiter, superwoman, astrologer, security guard, Eagle Scout, comedian, weatherperson, butterfly, pit bull, we, I, they, substitute teacher, hall monitor, boss, prisoner, clown, movie star, vampire, hair dresser, terrorist, preacher, senator, roller blader, cheater, astronaut, drummer, bus driver, detective, dolphin, surfer, snob, genius, mobster, lawyer, engineer, bodyguard

Category 2—Non-Living Things
Saturday, yoga, garden, finger, moon, ceremony, explosion, alphabet, cemetery, boombox, espresso machine, contact lens, paratrooper boot, Frisbee, Barbie doll, Walkman, soap opera, top-forty station, poetry, scar, karate, sandwich, cellulite, junk food, dreadlocks, lip gloss, SAT, PTA, garage, garbage, Porsche, dessert, Academy Award, UFO, nap, wave, brain, roller coaster, college, midnight, sushi, the White House

Category 3—Abstractions
stereotype, bravery, ignorance, display, publicity, poverty, schedule, common sense, reality, hysteria, The American Dream, trickery, prejudice, liberty, non-violence, sexism, dissent, possibility, vanity, truth, non-conformity, perfection, crime, gridlock, dishonesty, mediocrity, confidence, humor, fitness, secrecy, propaganda, happiness, belief, beauty, respectability, safety, awe, plan, efficiency, luck, oppression, envy, energy, morality, fame, hypocrisy, creativity, wealth

Verbs

break	coerce	destroy	symbolize
permit	escape	squelch	practice
skewer	tweak	poison	alter
shape	echo	appreciate	nag
transform	surround	scramble	despise
provoke	swat	skim	push
zap	save	build	escape
ooze	spike	generate	find
harass	humble	entertain	kill
mirror	predict	aggravate	defeat
cheer	idolize	honor	expose
spurn	gorge	excite	damage
dangle	dabble	check	silence
boost	imply	soothe	hasten
target	strip	float	adore
crack	tackle	forget	attract
unlock	replace	blur	offend
advance	delight	prefer	soothe
scatter	eye	scan	alter
coax	mock	hug	reward
squeeze	stain	recite	push
paw	blur	damage	agitate
spill	admit	puzzle	delight
anger	bar	delay	expose
wear	pooh-pooh	block	invent
produce			

Comment

Notice three categories of nouns: living things, non-living things, and abstract concepts. You can ask students to write three sentences, choosing subjects from each category. This allows them to compare and contrast the different types of sentences that different types of subjects generate.

If students compose their own lists, you'll want them to understand that all the verbs on the original list are transitive verbs: They take objects. This limitation is a way of pushing students to experiment with core sentences. However, you might now introduce them to intransitive verbs and change the rules to apply to those verbs which do not take direct objects.

2. Think Verbs

Powerful verbs can make you a more powerful writer. In revision, never allow a sentence to slip by in which you have not paid attention to the verb. Each of the writers below indulges in a verb extravaganza. Study the models, then try some similar paragraphs of your own.

> *To be governed is to have every opinion, every transaction noted, registered, counted, rated, stamped, measured, numbered, assessed, licensed, refused, authorized, endorsed, admonished, prevented, re-formed, redressed, corrected.*
> —Pierre Proudhoun, *The General Idea of the Revolution in the Nineteenth Century.*

> *Impossible dreams die hard. Like cartoon characters, they can be pulverized, poisoned, punctured, stomped flat, blown up, gut shot, cut into little pieces, dropped from high places, bludgeoned with a blunt instrument, fried to a crisp, boiled in oil, and buried at sea; and still they come back alive, whole, and grinning like homemade sin.*
> —Linda Ellerbee on, at seven-years-old, deciding to play third base for the New York Yankees

> *For years I have let dentists ride roughshod over my teeth; I have been sawed, hacked, chopped, whittled, bewitched, bewildered, tattooed, and signed on again; but this is cuspid's last stand.*
> —S. J. Perlman

Here are some sentence skeletons for starters:

- To be a high-school student is to be (pile up verbs)
- Good (or bad) things happen to those who _____.
  They can be (pile up verbs)
- Because I have_____, I have been (pile up verbs).

Essay

Should Schools Be Fragment-Free Zones?

I may be an English teacher, but this is no guarantee that sometimes I do not talk like a real person. On a bad day my speech is distinguished by enough false starts, hesitations, ninety-degree turns, and truncated sentences to satisfy a Professor Irwin Cory groupie. Relatives, students, and colleagues tolerate these bursts of semi-coherence in the same way a family at a holiday party puts up with the tasteless jokes of a kindly, but slightly drunk, bachelor uncle. "He's not always like that," they remind themselves.

Recently, however, confronted with a depressing transcript of my verbal fits and starts, I vowed to reform my meandering thoughts. Reversing that common and not always helpful advice—"Write like you talk"—I try now to talk more like I write.

Lately, however, I have been thinking more about how I got into this mess. Why this disconnect between my speaking and writing styles? During my formative years I did not know I had a problem. Teachers who themselves spoke in parsable sentences made sure my written prose conformed to the bloodless but clear school style of the era. At the same time, they tolerated, and were even sometimes entertained by, my faux-beatnik verbal ramblings. The idea that a group of spoken words should form a complete thought never occurred to me. My disjointed utterances, combined with inflections, gestures, and facial expressions, were the medium of my messages. Watching my own students punctuating with body language their "you knows" and "it was likes," I realize not much has changed. Writing is mostly a conscious activity, speech less so.

I am wondering what would happen if we were to promote complete sentences as a school priority. Everyone from the Superintendent of Schools to the Chalk Board Monitor would honor the union of subjects and predicates.

Who knows? Maybe the complete sentence idea will catch on big. It will be The Latest. Subjects and verbs will be right up there with baggy pants and hip hop. Should we hold our breath?

3. Experiment with Sentence Structure

You usually will not go wrong writing short sentences in which the subject and verb are right out front. The Andy Rooney Style may not excite, but it communicates:

> "When *I was* young, *I was* always ***having*** to do things *I hated*. ***School was*** harder than ***work has been***. *I liked* learning but ***found*** the process of education tedious. ***Staying up all night*** to study for an exam ***was*** a terrible experience, and *I did* it a lot in college. My ***parents*** and all the ***teachers said*** cramming didn't work but ***they were*** wrong. ***It may be*** the wrong way to learn but ***cramming is*** a good way to pass an exam. ***It*** just ***hurts*** a lot while ***you're doing*** it.
> —Andy Rooney, "Youth? You Can Have It"

The sentence structures here are clear and predictable. Some writers would try other, less obvious, possibilities, writing longer sentences that require the reader to wait around for the principal subject and verb.

The Rooney sentences could become:

> As a young man, always having to do things I hated, finding school harder than I later found work, loving learning but being bored with the tedious process of education, ***I crammed*** for college exams staying up late, acting against the advise of parents and teachers. ***Cramming***, even if the wrong way to learn and a terrible experience, ***is*** a good way to pass an exam. ***It*** just ***hurts*** while ***you're doing*** it.

But modern readers are not used to waiting around for the meaning of a sentence's subject, verb, and object. Previous generations have been more patient.

A British traveler reports on American table manners, 1829:

> The total want of the usual courtesies of table, the voracious rapidity with which the viands were seized and devoured, the strange

uncouth phrases and pronunciations, the loathsome spitting, from contamination of which it was absolutely impossible to protect our dresses; the frightful manner of feeding with their knives, till the whole blade seemed to enter the mouth, and the still more frightful manner of cleaning the teeth afterwards with a pocket knife, soon **forced us** [at last a verb and object] *to feel we were not surrounded by the generals, colonels, and majors of the old world, and that the dinner hour was to be anything rather than an hour of enjoyment.*
  —Frances Trollope, *Domestic Manners of the Americans,* 1829

Here is the way Frances Trollope might have presented these observations in a style more accessible to 1990s readers.

*When **I visited** America **I saw** some very bad table manners. **Americans** rapidly **seized** and **devoured** their food. When **they talked, they used** strange words and uncouth pronunciations. **We could** not **protect** our dresses from their loathsome spitting. They **ate** with their knives, putting the whole blade into their mouths. **We** soon **realized** that **we were** not **surrounded** by the generals, colonels, and majors of the old world. The **dinner hour was** to be anything but an hour of enjoyment.*

You can get practice expressing the same ideas in different sentence styles by writing a paragraph detailing changes in climate in your area over a typical year and the effect of these changes on the way people live. First write this account in direct sentences; then try it in suspended sentences that leave a lot of wiggle room between subject, verb, and object.

4. Try Packing a Sentence

The longer your sentence, the more likely it is to become unclear and ungrammatical. Still, once in a while, at least in the privacy of your journal, see how much you can load into one sentence without allowing it to collapse under the weight of too many modifying phrases and subordinate clauses.

Here British playwright Tom Stoppard explains cricket in one sentence:

> *It is a game played by two teams, of eleven players each, and one of these teams, going out to bat one at a time, attempts to score as many runs as possible while the other team, spreading itself around the field, attempts to limit these runs, a run being scored when a batsman strikes the ball sufficiently far to enable him to run twenty-two yards to the bowler's end of the pitch before the ball gets back there, unless the ball has been caught by a fielder before it bounces, in which case he is also out, and when both teams have had their turn, the team that has scored the most runs has won.*
> —*Home and Garden*

In a single sentence explain one of the following: the rules of a sport or game, the customs associated with a holiday, the organization of a political or social institution, the workings of a mechanical device—such as an internal combustion engine—or the stages in a legal or political process with which you are familiar (becoming a citizen, obtaining a driver's license). In working with this sentence, you can make use of participle phrases, (such as Stoppard's "going out to bat one at a time") and subordinators including:

▪ who	▪ because	▪ when	▪ except	▪ for
▪ which	▪ although	▪ that	▪ since	▪ unless
	▪ until	▪ if	▪ while	

Example:

How an American Political Party
Chooses a Presidential Candidate

The process by which an American political party chooses a presidential candidate culminates at a party convention in July or August of an election year, after beginning—sometimes as much as two years before the convention—when political hopefuls announce their intentions, then warming up in the spring of the election year when the field of candidates is narrowed through a series of state intra-party conventions, caucuses, or elections, the purpose of which is choose, according to a system based on state population, delegates to the national convention who, while committed to a particular candidate, are also willing to bargain, through what is sometimes a series of ballots, until a single candidate emerges with the minimum number of votes required by the party rules for nomination.

Accomplish your explanation with few, if any, "ands."

Comment

We are walking a thin line here. On the one hand, the student whose eyes light up at the opportunity to write an overcharged sentence generally should not be encouraged. Yet the challenge of making one ornately modified and subordinated sentence brings with it a chance to learn better how sentences work. Stress the importance of placing modifying and subordinating elements as close as possible to the part of sentence with which each connects.

Outlawing Whiches

THE semester's first set of papers tells me we have a problem here. It is the problem of the "whiches."

In high school I have not taken many of the courses I will need for the future, although I have taken some which maybe I can take at a later date.

The atmosphere of an eastern college will get me away from bad influences which I will benefit from greatly.

Looking at these sentences—and others like them—I review my alternatives. My choices are pretty much the same as they are when I confront any grammar and usage "vices."

- I can decriminalize their misuse.
- I can educate students to their hazards.
- I can selectively enforce penalties against offenders.
- I can ban them outright, announcing Draconian punishments for those foolhardy enough to flout the law.

The Argument for Decriminalization: Why make a big deal out of a minor illiteracy? Somebody says, "My sister gets better grades in biology which annoys me." I can take the time to ask in the margin, "What annoys you, biology or your sister's grades?" If my penmanship is legible, I will spend about fifteen seconds of my life writing out this comment. But, the truth is I *do* know what annoys her: her sister's higher grades in biology. My complaint is just an English teacher thing. Other people don't worry about these nit-picks.

The Argument for Education: OK. Maybe readers can decipher the meaning in sentences like these, but this kind of vagueness, habitually repeated, makes a reader uncomfortable. Part of a writer's job is to create user-friendly prose. I need to teach students to knock off these "whiches" from outer space. Meanwhile I should not penalize students for what I have not required them to learn.

The Argument for Selective Enforcement: Humane justice considers the circumstances of the offender and the severity of the offense. Consider a student who seems to be writing fewer sentences like, "I think that for happiness in life there is not too much related to money." Or: "My opinion about the importance of college could be that good grades are important to go." My job is to direct and encourage this student's progress in basic sentence structure, not jump all over him for a misplaced "which."

On the other hand, how about the boy with SAT scores high enough to set off the sort of college bidding war normally reserved for all-conference quarterbacks? I do not allow this student much wiggle room when he writes, "Apathetic citizens haven't studied the issues and may or may not vote, but sometimes they may, which makes the election seem meaningless." I am thinking (certainly hoping) that Princeton will not look kindly on such vagueness.

The Argument for an Outright Ban: I am staring at a stack of essays. But once again the rambling whiches are on the march. The mini-lessons are not working; the pleading comments are not working. Marlene writes, "As I got home my sister was baking a cake in the kitchen which was going to be a surprise for my birthday."

Monday morning I have an announcement: "No more 'whiches' in clauses tacked on to the end of sentences. NO MORE WHICHES," I repeat. I am warming to the topic, unleashing frustration that may have had more to do with low job status and a bad toothache than with vague pronouns. "The next paper with a 'which' clause tacked on to the end, GRAMMATICAL OR NOT, will be returned ungraded."

For about two weeks I wait. Nothing. My irrationality is paying off.

Then, "As Mr. X began to return our geometry papers, he let out no smiles, which, for him, was more than usual."

I know Mr. X. This is perfect. Monday morning I hear myself saying, "Remember what I said about 'whiches?' Well, we may need to allow some exceptions."

Essay

Picture Placement: Making Modifiers Visual

THE key principle of modification—place every word and phrase as close as possible to the word it describes or explains—is easy to learn, and, in practice, easy to forget. One way to focus attention on the results of modifiers that find themselves in the wrong place is to ask students to draw pictures illustrating the wayward modification. I have a collection of such sentences—some from student papers, some from newspapers and magazines—which I encourage students to make visual.

A student reads the sentence:

> *Lee's oldest son Mike signed a national letter of intent with Indiana University to play football for the Hoosiers in the family kitchen.*

She draws a picture of a uniformed wide receiver atop a kitchen stove reaching out for a pass.

Of course, not every modification error is appropriate for this activity. I save some for special occasions:

> *The French government is preparing television commercials encouraging the use of condoms that are blunt enough to shock even liberal Americans.*

Or the confusion on the Great Lover's bumper strip: *I Only Sleep with the Best.*

Here are some more sentences with which creative students have had fun.

Draw an illustration for:

> ▪ *Jefferson County Sheriff Wayne Hamilton this morning discussed the problems of lodging in the jail unconscious people*

suspected of being drunk with Jefferson County Commissioners."
—*Madison Courier*

or

- *Woman Hurt While Cooking Her Husband's Dinner in a Horrible Manner*

Some out-of-control modification invites humorous written response. I've asked students to compose an answer to this question on a college enrollment form: *Is English the best language you speak?*

And to this letter to the editor:

I should welcome information from any reader about the Leicester composer and musician, Benjamin Burrows, who died in 1966 to aid my research.
—Letter in *Musical Times*

I've encouraged students to debate whether or not the subject of the following letter of recommendation was fairly or unfairly denied employment based on the evidence of the letter: *I most enthusiastically recommend this candidate with no qualifications whatsoever.*

Of course, the best models for lessons in grammar and usage are student sentences in need of surgery. However, a teacher with a collection of professional bloopers can use these boo-boos to help students understand that blunders of this kind can embarrass writers long out of school. Anytime you can show a sixteen-year-old a way to avoid embarrassment, he or she will be listening.

5. Test Out Some Sentence Fragments

You can sometimes call attention to an idea by presenting it as a sentence fragment. In speech, people often seem able enough to communicate in clumps of words that aren't sentences. George Bush managed it when he was President:

Question: Mr. President, what does the Malta Summit mean?
Answer: Grandkids. All of that. Very important.

In an address urging the television industry to include anti-drug messages on Saturday cartoons: "Twenty million kids. Impressionable. Just asking to be entertained."

In writing, save your sentence fragments for surprising, ironic or emotional moments:

Cyra McFadden writes a tribute to her mother-in-law Ingrid McFadden: *I see her driving her two-tone Chevy, wearing her signature white gloves. I see her at the end of her life calm and courageous about dying. I remember her driving me to the church the day that I married her son.* **Lovely gesture. Wrong church. Vintage Ingrid.**
—*San Francisco Examiner*

Aging is like growing. It isn't a gradual imperceptible process, but happens in leaps and bounds. You can go for years being the same age. Your face doesn't change much; your weight remains the same. You never think of yourself as too old to learn the latest craze, can't wait to get off with the old and on to the new.

Then, crash. *You're polishing a mirror and you realize your neck has gone.* ***Just like that.*** *You put aside your polishing cloth and examine the thing that has appeared like a bracket joining your chin to your neck.* ***A wattle in fact.***
—Germaine Greer

Write a paragraph about a change in your life or about a person who is special to you. Try some appropriate sentence fragments.

6. Try Out Semi-Colons, Colons, Dashes

Move beyond a steady diet of periods and commas to other punctuation possibilities.

Study the sentence models below. Then think of a particular subject on which you are expert—a film, author, musical group, or athletic team. Limit your topic to *Dracula,* for example, not to "horror films." Then write sentences presenting opinions and information on this subject, using punctuation in some of the same ways as it is used in the model sentences.

Semi-Colons link closely related complete ideas within the same sentence.

> *We do not ride on the railroad; it rides upon us.* —Henry Thoreau, critiquing industrialism

> *Birds fly; fish swim; people gawk. It's mankind's Number 1 leisure activity. "Something's happening," says a voice as old as DNA deep within us, and we walk toward it.* —Jon Carroll, "In Defense of Gawking," *San Francisco Chronicle*

Colons show an equivalence between items on either side. The sentence preceding a colon should be complete.

> *I'm everything a real non-sexist person shouldn't be these days: a chair pusher, an elbow holder, a door-opener.* —Herb Caen

> *It wouldn't hurt for the Giants' fans to display something the (Giants) team has in abundance: class.* —Bill Mandel, *San Francisco Examiner*

> *There are two things no man will admit he can't do well: drive and make love.* —Sterling Moss, racing car driver

> *There's still a place in the world for men. Women want to be a lot of things traditionally considered masculine: doctors, rock stars,*

body builders, presidents of the United States. But there are plenty of masculine things women have, so far, shown no desire to be: pipe smokers, first-rate spin casters, wise old drunks, quiet. —P. J. O'Rourke, *Modern Manners*

Dashes provide a tool for punctuating asides, afterthoughts, and ironic commentary.

I like men to behave like men—strong and childish.
    —Françoise Sagan

On the elusive Greta Garbo: *When strangers met her over the years they often were—how could they not be—disappointed.*
    —Ellen Goodman

A prayer from the young St. Augustine: *Give me chastity—but not yet.*

Essay

The Sentence Treasure Hunt: Teaching Sentence Variety

AS a teacher of sentence structure, my first job is to lead students to a relationship with sentences composed of clear subjects linked to precise active verbs. Then it's time to help them find ways to spice up these basic nutrients.

One way I do this is with the Sentence Treasure Hunt. During a class period, students visit the school library in teams to find and record sentences that conform to a particular grammatical structure. I give them models. For example:

1. **A sentence containing a noun appositive**

   Mr. Jones, *the only civics teacher in our school who can recite the Bill of Rights backwards,* jogs daily.

2. **A "which" clause separating subject and verb**

   His jogs, *which allow him a solitary chance to practice this unusual skill,* take place before sunrise.

3. **A compound verb**

   This regimen, Jones believes, *builds* the body and *trains* the mind.

4. **An adjective appositive following a noun**

   When Jones organized a student club to promote his technique for developing physical and mental fitness, a group of parents, *shocked and indignant,* protested.

5. **An "-ing" participial phrase separating the subject and the verb**

   These parents, *clutching copies of the Constitution and waving American flags,* descended on the principal's office.

6. **Dashes setting off a parenthetical expression**

They claimed—*not without justification*—that students should learn to understand the Bill of Rights before memorizing it backwards.

7. **An "ed" participial phrase separates the subject and verb**

The principal, *trapped by his desire to please everyone,* just smiled.

8. **A sentence containing a colon**

Finally, a thoughtful member of the parents' group suggested a compromise: the students in Mr. Jones' club would recite the Bill of Rights forward while jogging backwards.

9. **Two participial phrases introducing the subject**

Encouraged by this spirit of compromise and *hoping to put the matter behind him,* the principal endorsed this plan.

10. **A sentence fragment**

And Jones?

11. **A three- or four-word subject-verb-object sentence**

No one asked Jones.

12. **A rhetorical question**

Does this surprise you?

An alternative to The Treasure Hunt would be to ask students to use some of these sentence forms—not necessarily in the order used here—to write an original connected narrative.

7. Write Balanced Sentences

You've probably learned the basic principle of parallel structure—
that grammatical forms within a sentence need to correspond.

> **Not:** I disliked him because he was selfish (adjective) and be-
> cause of his lechery (noun).
> **But:** I disliked him because he was selfish and lecherous (or
> because of his selfishness and lechery).

Some writers, however, go beyond this basic rule, using the concept
of parallel forms to write artfully balanced sentences which, while they
may seem a little stiff for, say, chatting it up on a first date, are an important tool of many who write rhythmic, ear-pleasing prose.

Read these sentences and choose the word from the list on the next
page that fits each blank. The word you choose should be consistent
with the meaning and grammatical structure of the sentence.

> *The various modes of worship which prevailed in the Roman
> world were all considered by the people as equally true, by the phi-
> losophers as equally* _____ *and by the magistrates as equally*
> _____. —Edmund Gibbon

> *History is an account, mostly false, of events mostly*
> _____, *which are brought about by rulers, mostly knaves,
> and soldiers, mostly* _____. —Ambrose Bierce

James I on the evils of smoking: *A custom loathsome to the
eye,* _____ *to the nose, harmful to the brain,* _____
to the lungs.

Hollywood manager Jay Bernstein on his career as a celebrity representative: *I think the most poetic way of putting it is that*

when I got them to where they wanted to be, the air became rarefied, they became _____, and I became _____.

When in doubt, _____; when in trouble, delegate; when in charge, _____. —James Boren, American bureaucrat

In war, resolution; in defeat, _____; in victory, _____. —Winston Churchill

The Words

- mumble
- deified
- false
- fools

- nullified
- hateful
- ponder
- magnanimity

- defiance
- unimportant
- dangerous
- useful

Answers: Gibbon—*false, useful.* Bierce—*unimportant, fools.* James I—*hateful, dangerous.* Bernstein—*deified, nullified.* Boren—*mumble, ponder.* Churchill—*defiance, magnanimity.*

---

8. Repeat Words to Build Unity and Emotion

Your English teacher is right. "Cucumber" as the subject—or object—of three sentences in a row probably makes for a choppy, tedious style. But don't interpret this caution to mean that repetition is always bad form. You can repeat words within paragraphs and, indeed, within sentences, to create rhythm and build unity.

Occasionally, you can even generate emotional tingles with a series of clauses or phrases by repeating words. Save this technique for times you are out to raise blood pressure as well as consciousness. But don't be afraid to try this repetition.

Examples:

Man's destructive hand spares nothing that lives; he kills to feed himself, he kills to clothe himself, he kills to adorn himself, he kills to attack, he kills to defend himself, he kills to instruct himself, he kills to amuse himself, he kills for the sake of killing.
—Josef De Maistre

What does labor want? We want more schoolhouses and less jails; more books and less arsenals; more learning and less vice; more leisure and less greed; more justice and less revenge; in fact, more of the opportunities to cultivate our better natures, to make manhood more noble, womanhood more beautiful, childhood more happy and bright.
—Samuel Gompers, labor leader

Damn the bright lights by which no one reads, damn the continuous music no one hears, damn the grand pianos that no one can play, damn the white houses mortgaged up to their gutter, damn them for plundering the ocean for fish to feed the mink whose skins they wear, and damn their shelves on which there rests a single book—a copy of the telephone directory bound in brocade.
—John Cheever, *The New Yorker*

Written for Valentine's Day: *We have seen them sleeping slack-mouthed, eyelids twitching like dreaming cats; we have seen them bolt upright, muscles tight, eyes wide with pleasure. We have seen them awkward and graceful; we have seen them reaping and sowing.*

But just when we think that we have discovered all the some-things about them there is something else. Valentine's Day would be a pointless holiday for us were it not for that.

Were it not for the unknown at the center of the known.

Were it not for the pulse of the blood under our hand.

Were it not for the embrace of the longtime lover.

—Jon Carroll, *San Francisco Chronicle*

An Englishman does everything on principle: he fights you on patriotic principles; he robs you on business principles; he enslaves you on imperial principles.

—George Bernard Shaw

Consider your most passionately held belief. Defend it, as the writers of these paragraphs do, by making use of emotion-generating repetition.

9. Juxtapose Opposites

Create tension in your sentences by pairing opposites. The result may be funny, dramatic, or paradoxical.

Newspaper columnist Herb Caen on socialite parties: *People with face**lifts dropping** names and **picking up** gossip.*

*If a man hasn't discovered something he will **die** for, he isn't fit to **live**.* —Martin Luther King

*The **less** a statesman amounts to, the **more** he loves the flag.* —Frank Hubbard

*Socialism seeks to **pull down** wealth; liberalism seeks to **raise up** poverty.* —Winston Churchill

On the sixties generation: *Never ... was any generation ... intent upon the pursuit of happiness more advantageously placed to attain it who yet, with seeming deliberation, took the opposite course—towards **chaos**, not **order**, towards **breakdown**, not **stability**, toward **death, destruction** and **darkness**, not **life, creativity** and **light**.* —Malcolm Muggeridge, *Esquire*

*The Puritans hated bear baiting not because it gave **pain** to the bear, but because it gave **pleasure** to the spectator.* —Thomas Macaulay, *History of England*

*Never **underestimate** a man who **overestimates** himself.* —Franklin D. Roosevelt on Douglas MacArthur

*To yield is to be preserved whole. To be **bent** is to become **straight**.* —Lao Tzu

*Poetry **lies** its way to the **truth**.* —John Ciardi

Less** is **more. —Mies van der Rohe, architect

*The most **incomprehensible** thing about the world is that it is **comprehensible**.* —Albert Einstein

*A nation is only at **peace** when it is at **war**.* —Hugh Kingsnell

Here are some opposites that invite juxtaposition. Fool around with placing them in the same sentence, and you may generate some ideas you didn't know you had:

- eloquent—mute
- sharp—blunt
- chaste—promiscuous
- choose—reject
- honor—disgrace
- pliant—stiff
- illusion—reality
- ignorant—informed
- sudden—gradual
- genuine—fake
- vulgar—tasteful
- flower—wilt
- flatter—insult
- clarify—confuse
- conquered—victorious
- greedy—generous
- devious—direct
- mandatory—voluntary
- strict—lenient
- essential—incidental
- true—false
- by chance—by design
- harmony—dissonance
- pure—polluted
- pampered—neglected
- conformity—eccentricity
- curious—apathetic
- punish—reward
- free—restrain
- credulous—suspicious
- infinite—limited

PART VI: WRITERS LOVE WORDS

- **What the Dictionary Doesn't Tell You:**
  Seven Ways to Explore Diction

- **Poetry in Prose:**
  Nine Ways to Sharpen Your Metaphors

- **Fun and Games for Serious Writers:**
  Seven Ways to Play with Words

WRITERS LOVE WORDS

WHAT THE DICTIONARY DOESN'T TELL YOU:
SEVEN WAYS TO EXPLORE DICTION

Essay

GHOULISH as it may seem, I sometimes fantasize about the little eulogies loved ones might offer at my funeral. In one scenario I picture a friend intoning a list of words I would not have been caught dead using—no pun intended.

Part of the catalogue would go like this:

When asked to make a decision, he did not answer, "Whatever."

He never tried to endear himself to his students by using the language of Wayne's World.

He did not call a drink a "beverage" or make a serious case for "quality time."

He made a point to use sparingly the "ism" words—"racism," "sexism," "ageism," and the others—as a little protest against those who use them too often and too indiscriminately.

For the most part, he left words like "Eros," "zeitgeist," and "intentionality" to assistant professors.

And, to the end, he refused to use "impact" as a verb.

These are some of the verbal quirks and biases that are my language biography. I've given a lot of thought to the words I want to speak for me. The workouts in this section will help others, also, choose words that better reflect who they want to be.

1. Visualize Words

Think not only of the dictionary definition of a word but also of its connotations—the pictures, thoughts, and emotions that the word carries with it.

What, for instance, are the differences in connotation between "environmentalist" and "eco-freak"?

"Environmentalist" evokes Volvos with Save the Whales bumper strips, Sierra Club coffee table books, backpacking in the Grand Tetons.

"Eco-freak" induces images of tree spiking, tie-dye, green flags, rhetoric-filled meetings, manifestos.

Detail the pictures projected by some of the following sets of related words. What do you see?

- the first day of school
- the last day of school

- Honda motorcycle
- Harley Davidson

- elder
- elderly person

- Wonder Bread
- Good Earth nine grain bread

- the letter "X"
- the letter "Z"

- minorities
- people of color

- quiche
- omelet

- dance
- ball

- AM radio
- FM radio

- Negro
- African American

- teenager
- adolescent

- teacher
- educator

- idealist
- do-gooder

What's in a Name?:
Playing with Connotations of Proper Nouns

PROPER names come packed with connotations. "Hilda" suggests blonde braids and dumpy dresses. "Debbie" is silky Clairol tresses and Guess jeans. I have used names to discuss with students the subtexts words can summon, a technique that worked well enough unless a Hilda or Debbie actually turned up in my classroom, at which time things got sticky.

So I have learned to yield the floor to that all-time champion of resonant names, Charles Dickens. I give students a Dickensian name like Captain Boldwig and ask them, with no further information, to write a paragraph describing this character's appearance, occupation, "lifestyle," and temperament. Then I ask students to share and compare the associations they would get from these names. Sometimes, with the less easily intimidated, I read aloud some of the character sketches in *The Pickwick Papers*.

- Horatio Fizkin, Esquire
- Anthony Hummm
- Alfred Jingle
- Henrietta Nupkins
- Mr. Phunkey
- Dr. Slammer
- Mr. Guppy
- Mr. Jellyby
- Mr. Murdstone
- Lady Dedlock
- Ms. Flite
- Mr. Slurk
- Mr. Smangle
- The Hon. Samuel Slumkey
- Mr. Raddle
- Morlenna Kenwigs
- Wackford Squeers
- Ninetta Crummles
- Brothers Cherryble
- Mr. Turveydrop
- Mr. Toots
- Rev. Mr. Stiggins

2. Consider Your Options

Keep reminding yourself that there are many ways to say the same thing. Here are four different translations of a single sentence from the *Odyssey.* Odysseus has just outwitted the monstrous Cyclops. He says:

Joy touched my secret soul. (Pope)
I was filled with laughter. (Fitzgerald)
I chuckled to myself. (Rieu)
And my heart laughed. (Mandelbaum)

"Four score and seven years ago" could have been (but, thankfully, is not) "Eighty-seven years ago."

Find a paragraph in a classic work of literature. Rewrite it two different ways.

Essay

Couch Potato Research: Not Learning Is Not Easy

FILM provides our best record of comparison between how people have talked Then and Now. This fact opens an avenue of research for students who like to space out with old movies on TV. They can collect the language of an earlier time.

One student, focusing only on terms of enmity and endearment, managed to resurrect, using no tool more sophisticated than a remote control, "impudent knave," "dirty cuss," "big galoot," "sly rascal," "young whippersnapper," "little dickens," "pesky varmint," "lamb chop," "honey bun," and "goofus."

Students take from this activity a better understanding of the vital and changing nature of language and also, I hope, some sense that if they pay attention they can always learn, even when they are ostensibly kicking back.

3. Know the Difference Between Sweet Words and Sour Words

Remember the words you choose affect your message at least as strongly as the logic of your message. Yogi Berra understood this: "I ain't in no slump, I just ain't hitting," he said.

Consider:

- After the hometown wins a football championship, excited fans start fires and turn over cars. Are the fans "vandals" or "merrymakers"?
- When people you don't like win a dispute, do you say they "hail" their victory or "gloat over" it?
- Is an anti-abortion court decision a "major setback for abortion rights" or a "major victory for abortion opponents"?
- Should the presenters at the Academy Awards ceremony say, "The Oscar goes to … " rather than "The winner is … "?
- Does a marriage "break up" or "dissolve"?
- Does one "sue" or "file" for divorce?
- Is somebody with money "a person of means" or a "fat cat"?
- Do politicians have "friends" or "cronies"? "Followers" or "stooges"?
- Is what happened on the school playground "a race riot" or "a scuffle in which the kids on one side happened to be Hispanic and the other kids happened to be African American"?

Below are some sentences which try to use neutral language. Rewrite a couple of them twice, creating a positive and negative version. Rely primarily on nouns and verbs, rather than adjectives and adverbs.

It's OK to exaggerate, but when you do, the sentences may come out a little overheated. Think of this challenge as word play, practice in manipulating language. When writing for real, an over-the-top deluge of loaded words may make you appear high-spirited but irrational—or, at least, overly enthusiastic.

Example: Students at our school attend classes daily.

Positive: Each day, young people at our school have the opportunity to seek out educational adventures.

Negative: Day after day, kids at this school must drag themselves through a tedious regimen of mandatory lectures.

1. My dog plays with any object he finds. (Make the dog look good, then bad.)

2. Many of this year's movies are similar to those that made a profit last year. (Make the movies look good, then bad.)

3. In class, we took notes, asked questions, and supplied answers. (Make these activities sound positive, then negative.)

4. Our city depends on the revenue it makes entertaining visitors. (Make this activity seem positive, then negative.)

5. Television provides viewers with news, information, and entertainment. (Make television look good, then bad.)

4. Hear Beautiful Words

As with musical notes, word syllables produce sounds that, in combination, are pleasing or harsh to the ear. Some words, like "summer day" and "check enclosed," make us feel good because of thoughts they inspire, but other words, like "whippoorwill" and "chameleon," sound good to many people irrespective of their definition and connotations. But can we agree on which words produce beautiful sounds? In an informal poll, people consistently (with, of course, some variation from person to person) chose twenty-one "beautiful words" from the list of forty-eight words below. Make your selections and compare your list with others. Now make your own list of beautiful-sounding words.

I	II	III	IV	V	VI
lullaby	lupine	clamor	grease	pejorative	iridescent
filigree	voluptuous	liver	bowling	jukebox	sumptuous
charade	unguent	gamble	intercom	hygiene	wisteria
sultry	panacea	bamboozle	gall	squat	lassitude
pirouette	debonair	fuzz	vegetable	spatter	suave
mosaic	sapphire	penchant	bungle	slaughter	innuendo
carousel	lagoon	funk	dentist	accessory	languorous
barley	bushwhacker	awkward	dog	fax	hamburger

Comment

The most commonly selected beautiful words are the first seven words in columns one, two, and six.

5. Know the Difference Between Funny and Unfunny Words

Have you noticed the mere mention of some words can make people laugh while other similar words won't even bring a forced smile?

"Cigar" is funny. You think of the little plutocrat in the pinstriped trousers in the monopoly set and expressions like "close but no cigar" and smirky, phallic references. "Cigarette," however, has none of these smile-inducing qualities and, more than anything, connotes cancer and death.

Here are some pairs of funny, not funny words:

Not Funny	**Funny**
England	Liechtenstein
tights	pantyhose
oil	gas
Science Diet	Kibbles n' Bits
Jeopardy	Let's Make a Deal
April 15	April 1
tomato	rutabaga
astronomy	astrology
Latin	Pig Latin
Harvard	Chico State
Martin Luther King Day	Groundhog Day

Continue this list. Think about the images you associate with each word.

6. Manipulate Euphemisms

Euphemisms, those agreeable expressions that disguise the unpleasant, can be irritating, even dangerous, when they allow us to shrug off events and conditions that should seriously concern us. The planner who labels the future world in which crowded millions starve a "biosphere overload" makes this scary state of affairs sound like no more than a computer malfunction. Even if we aren't sure what Fidel Castro means when he introduces "the campaign for the rectification of errors and negative tendencies," we can be pretty sure from the euphemistic sound of the words that he is up to no good. And a laid-off worker's pain is not eased when she is told she is being given a "career change opportunity." These slimy examples are real, the handiwork of well-paid, if misguided, professionals.

But not all euphemisms are contemptible. Some merely sweeten the unpleasant. It's OK to buffer the reality by explaining to your finicky aunt that your dog just had an "accident" on her Persian carpet.

Most euphemisms are not so much immoral as phony. "Administrative assistants compensated for their efforts" are still "secretaries paid for their work." And the "song stylists featured in lounges" remain "singers working barrooms."

We learn to read between the lines. A boss hiring someone whose recommendation letter credits him with "meticulous attention to detail" should know she may get an insufferable nitpicker.

The person who answers a personal ad placed by a "dynamic" individual had better be prepared for "pushy."

Euphemisms are sometimes just a way of being polite. Write a polite note of advice to an acquaintance letting the person know that others find him or her scatterbrained, wimpy, loud, self-centered, sloppy, oversensitive, reclusive, boring, neurotic, or sex-obsessed. Or several of the above. Use none of these blunt words. Be positive and supportive without being cloying.

Simple and Direct Made Difficult

WHY does Mr. Warriner of the *Grammar and Usage Handbook* wimp out when the going gets rough?

Warriner, like other arbiters of correctness, insists on the established distinctions, the difference between "affect" and "effect," and between "good" and "well," and on and on. But, fussy as they are, Warriner and his fellow rulemakers will seldom favor "stop" over " desist," or "desire" over "desirous." Teachers who promote simple and direct prose don't always get help.

Among the barriers we face are books with titles like *500 Pretentious Words to Boost Your SAT Score*. While, of course, we want to encourage students to learn as many words as possible any way they can, they should also understand that Big Words don't always make for muscular prose.

A student writes, "At a recent student dance, chaperones felt an obligation to call in police in order to terminate an affray."

I say, "The police came to break up a brawl."

He says, "Those are junior high school words, and besides they sound kind of crude."

"Right," I say, "a brawl is kind of crude." I tell him, in so many words, that this report of an incident at a school dance is not the format in which to come on like James Fenimore Cooper.

This is how it has gone. Much of my job has been spent trying to take the hot air out of student prose, to help students understand the difference between an educated style and a pompous one.

Of course, those who have just learned the word "facilitate" are not eager to settle for "bring about," and it is true that "to apprise" does sound a lot more college prep than "to tell."

So, I've pulled back from little lectures on the power of Anglo Saxon. Now, as the challenges in this section illustrate, I encourage students to listen to the sound, vibrations and connotations of words. I'm hoping, maybe against hope, that the future managers among them will someday tell their subordinates "to carry out a workable plan" rather than "effect a viable stratagem."

7. Say It Your Way, Not the Newspaper's Way

Read newspapers, listen to the news, but don't let the language of reporters and news analysts prompt your word choices. Journalists rely on a predictable set of terms and phrases which help them do their job, words which sound canned and mass-produced when others borrow them.

News analysts report on "grave misgivings." Ordinary people "have their doubts."

Predictably, most every journalistic analysis of California includes the word "dream," even if the dream is "tarnished." Likewise, in the world of newspaper language, a "speculation" will always be "fueled," and a tumor removed during an operation will be the size of a "golf ball" or an "orange," never a "travel alarm clock."

On the editorial page, problems always seem to be "deeply rooted" and "multifaceted," having "profound implications."

Even when your ideas are influenced by journalists, you do not have to regurgitate journalese. Find a piece of news analysis or an editorial on a subject that interests you. Read the piece, then put it aside and summarize it in your words and your own style.

Is That Your Own Tired, Overused Expression or Someone Else's?

MOST of us who work with student writers understand Samuel Goldwyn's plaintive call: "What we need is some new clichés." Ah, to never again read of a drink that hit the spot or of the vacation trip on a highway flat as a pancake. Many of us try to minimize the pain by building students' cliché awareness.

But I want to write here about a teacher with a different take on clichés. To her, an abundance of clichés in student writing is not a sign of an immature style but of a style that is suspiciously too mature. She views an excess of hackneyed phrases in a paper as a telltale sign of "outside help." The Three Cliché Rule is her benchmark: If, in a theme of five hundred words, three or more full-grown clichés appear, the student writer could be in big trouble.

However, unlike other of her rules, such as the "no sentences beginning with a conjunction" rule, the three cliché rule is a little fuzzy, forcing her to face the irritating question, "What is a cliché?" In specific cases, on the mistaken assumption that my own insubstantial knowledge on this subject may be greater than hers, she'll ask my opinion.

"How about this one? 'Preach to the converted.' Do kids talk like that?"

"What do you think about 'the almighty dollar?' My mother used to say that. Have you ever heard a sixteen-year-old say 'the almighty dollar'?"

I try to answer these questions, but what I am really thinking is, "Why are you giving yourself an ulcer?" I make gentle suggestions. If she is really so concerned about outside help, she should have students write papers in class or assign papers on topics kids know more about than their family members, or—the ultimate heresy—encourage students to get help with their writing from anyone willing to offer it. Then, at the same time, she could fling this Three Cliché Rule out in the open so whole families are aware of its existence. Who knows? She might touch off a multi-generational search for a lively and alternative way to say, "That's water over the dam," or "It's time to get down to brass tacks."

My War Against Vacuity: Reports from the Front

I have always believed that part of being an English teacher is to commit oneself, like some word-crazy Don Quixote, to the quest for an illusionary world, free of vague, evasive, impenetrable, and otherwise empty language.

It is not, however, always easy to enlist students in this crusade against verbal vapidity.

I remember, for example, returning to my class from one of those "professional growth" days on which teachers who have not had the good sense to call in sick are held captive by big-money, easy-answer consultants. I found myself in a locked room with one particular "expert" who told us: "You must overcome your belief barriers and be energy focused. You and your students need to be in a high-learning mode."

These condescending noises made me so angry I copied his exact words to pass on to my students, and the next day I faced a class saying, "See how we are made to spend time on these so-called 'professional growth days.' I was trapped with a guy making probably $1,000 a day who was oozing emptiness like ... " Then I quoted his inanities.

A long and unsympathetic silence ensued, broken finally by a question from the class entrepreneur, a boy who had made a killing selling videotapes of his middle school graduation ceremony. "How much did you say that guy made?" he asked.

In my ardor to rally the troops in the fight against empty language, I once even stooped to picking on the much maligned Dan Quayle.

"Look," I said. "Here's Dan Quayle's deep thinking on education: 'Quite frankly, teachers are the only profession that teach our children.'"

I expected that students would have an easy laugh, sniggering at this evidence of non sequiturs in high places. What I got was basically a shrug. The shrug said, "Hey, talk like this doesn't matter because no one is really listening."

So I've tried to bend a little. I remind myself that when some P.R. person posing as insider writes a sentence like, "Golf could well continue its current wonderful surge, or it could fall on evil times," he is not constructing this quintessential emptiness for the sole purpose of driving me crazy.

I have learned that people can get passionate when their favorite prattle is challenged. I once made the mistake of holding up to ridicule—in a lesson on shaky pronoun references—the words of New Age entrepreneur Werner Erhard: "What I recognized is that you can't put it together. It's already together and what you have to do is experience it being together."

I suppose I should not have been surprised when I received a three-page, typed, single-spaced letter from a parent and EST graduate that attempted to explain Erhard and attack me in language as incomprehensible as the guru's own. Unfortunately, I found these insults no less disconcerting because they were delivered in psychobabble.

So the going has sometimes been rough for stalwarts in the fight for prose that actually says something. In addition to the politicians and self-promoters, the empty words of advertisers are everywhere. Bright young people are well paid for writing sentences like: "You are the new coffee generation, because coffee lets you calm yourself down and pick yourself up. Coffee gives you the serenity to dream it and the vitality to do it."

Add to this social tolerance of hollow words the natural attraction the young feel for abstractions and the teacher who demands verbal exactness can come off as a language killjoy. Young people at a certain stage of learning fall in love with free-floating words. I, myself, remember long ago hours spent in coffee houses pondering essentially meaningless (as I now see them) propositions like, "There is no effect and cause, there is only cause and effect." I can recall once writing a poem which included the words, "Let us immerse ourselves in the great reservoir of transcendence."

So given the forces, natural and manufactured, blocking the arrival of the Utopia of Lucid Language, why do some of us keep ranting about the importance of clear, or at least penetrable, prose?

Here's an explanation of one kind: A couple of years ago I read a comment from the actress Annette Bening's press secretary, who was not further identified. This person had been asked whether or not Ms. Bening had given birth to a child. The answer was, "The determination to make a statement has not been cleared." Reading this, I felt a curious satisfaction. I calculated that in thirty years of teaching I had tried to pressure, prod, and cajole as many as eight thousand students toward clear writing. I was confident—even beyond what the mathematical odds might justify—that none of these people was working as a spokesperson for Annette Bening.

Essay

Making Poetry Without a License:
The Novice Writer's Need to Experiment

MEGAN writes, "To me, reading *Great Expectations* was sort of like reading a giraffe. It was long and mostly it was kind of washed out and boring, but there were quite a few interesting spots."

I am staggered by this absurdly creative simile. How does anyone, least of all a fifteen-year-old devoted to the predictability of Sweetwater High novels, find the inventiveness to link a giraffe and a book? I love this kind of imaginative spunk. My perfect world would be inhabited by a high percentage of creative people willing to risk the hoots of others.

However, I am also an English teacher employed by the citizens of the City and County of San Francisco. In this capacity, I am being paid to tell Megan—as gently as possible, perhaps—that her analogy makes little sense. Without putting too fine a point on it, giraffes are not "long" in the same way that books are "long," and to compare a giraffe's spots and a book's "interesting spots" is charming but mind-boggling.

Although the taxpayers of the City and County may expect me to point all this out to Megan, they are going to have to find someone else to do their dirty work. I am leaving Megan alone for awhile with her right-brainy disconnections. I may even praise effusively her creativity. Should she continue to contrive these beautiful if sputtering figures of speech, I will then start to talk to her about making the elements mesh.

But not yet. Rather, I am going to allow students to sometimes enter a world where writing can be a Jules Feiffer Dance to Creativity performed on a field without fences. A beginning writer should be able to try out a few uncertain moves without being required to execute first a perfect arabesque.

The writing workouts in this section encourage students to experiment with similes, metaphors, and analogies.

1. Be Poetic Sometimes

Just because you are writing non-fiction prose is no reason to be prosaic. Sometimes jump beyond the literal definition of words.

Each of the following is a collection of fanciful descriptions for a common natural phenomenon. What is being described in each group?

Example: a blackout, a dropped shudder (Beryl Markham), glistening caviar (Diane Wakoski), the dive of one great crow (Richard Wilbur). **Answer:** Nightfall

1. vast castles, blue animals stampeding (George Garrett), snowcapped mountains
2. suds in a pan (Helen Hudson), great boneless white birds (Hugh Walpole), milk spilt on a blue table (F. van Wyck Mason)
3. clear falling beads, an explosion in a glass factory (T. Coraghessan Boyle) silver needles (Frank Swinnerton)
4. yellow snow, (Susan Engberg), neglected toys on the grass (Carolyn Slaughter), a soggy brown blanket
5. shower of white confetti, uncooked grains of rice (Marge Piercy), quiet feathers (H. E. Bates)
6. diamond lamps (Hans Christian Andersen), winking eyes, (William Humphrey) the lights of far off ships. (Marjory Stoneman Douglas)

See some of the following phenomena fancifully rather than literally: the sun, trees bending in a wind storm, the first blossoms of spring, a leafless tree in winter, a waterfall, snow melting, sunset at midsummer, a bolt of lightning, a formation of migrating birds.

Comment

Answers: (1) waves, (2) clouds, (3) falling rain drops, (4) leaves on the ground, (5) snow flakes, (6) stars

---

2. Connect Qualities and Things

You can experiment with similes by making lists of objects which share the same quality. Begin by extending the following lists with more examples for each adjective. Stay away from expressions you recognize as clichés. (Sharp as a tack.)

small as
- a bread crumb
- a snail
- a grain of rice
- a snowflake

thin as
- tracing paper
- prison broth
- piano wire
- a cobweb

alone as
- a scarecrow
- a planet
- a lighthouse
- an island

soft as
- old money
- butter
- cat fur
- yarn

empty as
- a tree branch in winter
- a casket in a mortuary sales room
- an air balloon
- a new diary

silent as
- fog
- a fish
- dust settling
- a held breath

3. Work for Exactness in Comparisons

Play with similes and metaphors until you are satisfied the parts mesh. As you match the two parts of the similes below you should find only one precise coupling for each pair. An asterisk (*) next to the term on the left means that the comparison is a negative one (sensitive as cement).

1. highly seasoned*   a. as the expression of a farm boy at a Latin lesson
2. quiet   b. as a spider making a web
3. reckless*   c. as a cork leaving a champagne bottle
4. blank   d. as a bus driver's sock
5. bald   e. as a toothbrush
6. alluring*   f. as a tongue depressor
7. abrupt   g. as a Xerox
8. original*   h. as grapefruit
9. private   i. as a night watchman with arthritis

Let these models inspire you to work out similes for some of the following descriptive words: agile, aloof, angry, busy, careless, calm, clean, confident, conspicuous, depressed, delicate, dignified, flustered, graceful, greedy, inflexible, lonely, pompous, subtle.

Comment

Answers and Sources: 1. **f** (Ross Macdonald) 2. **b** (Honore de Balzac) 3. **i** (Raymond Chandler) 4. **a** (Raymond Chandler) 5. **h** (Raymond Chandler) 6. **d** (Victoria Wood) 7. **c** (P. G. Wodehouse) 8. **g** (Laurence J. Peter) 9. **e** (O. Henry)

Essay

What Is Good Writing?: The Short Answer

I enjoy art, but I don't much like to give opinions about it. Any judgments I might make about, say, a Jackson Pollack are private, more or less capricious, and difficult to articulate.

But judging writing is not like that. Good writing is not a matter of "Hey, whatever turns you on." Good writing (with allowance for geniuses who go their own way) is—for starters—economical, vivid, clear, appropriate, and sometimes surprising.

Figures of speech, because they are by definition condensed, provide concise illustrations of writing which, according to the above criteria, does and doesn't work.

Here are some samples from my collection.

Good writing is economical:

The peaceful population is a sea in which the guerrilla swims like a fish. —Mao Zedong

Things are in the saddle and ride mankind. —Ralph Waldo Emerson

Bad writing is overly complicated:

Ronald Reagan writes to departing White House Aide Michael Deaver: *We consider (your) leaving in the nature of an amputation. You will continue to be part of our lives. We will have concern for the other, and refuse surgery that would in anyway remove you from a relationship that is part of our life-support system.*

Good writing is vivid:

I do not see the European Economic Community as a great love affair. It is more like nine middle-aged couples with failing marriages meeting at Brussels hoping for a group grope. —E. P. Thompson, peace activist, 1975.

Bad writing is clouded:

People want the bricks of government to function. —Diane Feinstein

Good writing is appropriate:

We have to combat the wolf of socialism, and we shall be able to do it far more effectively as a pack of hounds than as a flock of sheep. —Winston Churchill

Bad writing is inappropriate:

On "intellectual adolescence" among Democrats: *It's like our policies are pimples on the face of Democratic politics. Our job is to apply ointment on a hormonally confused party.* —David Skaggs, congressional representative from Colorado

From a book about cooking with leftovers: *Making herbed butter for unexpected guests is a fine example of emergency cuisine that works like clean underwear in a car wreck.*

Good writing is fresh and surprising:

A woman without a man is like a fish without a bicycle —feminist graffiti

Bad writing is often cliché-drenched:

We are cutting off our noses to spite our faces and this leaves us very shortsighted. —Dr. Dean Edell, media doctor

4. Try for Fresh Similes

Work for similes which are free of clichés. Not "happy as a dog with a bone" or "happy as a clam," rather "happy as a ten-year-old on June 15th."

Ten of the similes below are overused expressions. Find them and convert them to original similes.

1. Neat as a pin
2. Old as Methuselah
3. Mad as a wet hen
4. Hungry as a horse
5. Smart as a whip
6. Guilty as sin
7. Naked as rain
8. Quiet as a mouse
9. Free as the breeze
10. Easy as trying to paint the wind
11. Easy as falling off a log
12. Smooth as the nose of a moth
13. Dark as the inside of a cow
14. Scared as a jackrabbit
15. Thin as linguini
16. Intimate as the rustle of sheets
17. Rare as rocking horse manure
18. Nervous as a cricket on a crowded floor

Comment

Original similes—7. Wallace Stevens, 10. Anonymous, 12. Karl Shapiro, 13. Mark Twain, 15. Anonymous, 16. Dorothy Parker, 17. Anonymous, 18. Ross Macdonald

Working to inoculate young writers against the virus of tired language is a difficult task. First of all, they are about as concerned with avoiding clichés as they are with lowering their cholesterol counts. In addition, some may never have heard the expression "free as a breeze" before undertaking this workout. However, even the cliché-illiterate should recognize a freshness in "dark as the inside of a cow" that is lacking from "hungry as a horse."

5. Use Similes and Metaphors to Evoke Physical Features and Voices

Practice creating similes and metaphors by observing faces and bodies and listening to voices and asking, "What does this remind me of?"

[Robin Williams has] *a razor-slash nose like a tired mouse, tiny mad eyes as blue as anti-freeze. And enough hair on his flailing arms to stuff an elk . . . 'My God,' Robin barks like a demented seal, off and running at the mouth like a power hose at a race riot.*
—Brad Dart, *People*

A look around the bar gave you a close-up of Faces from Hell— faces made out of old throw rugs, faces cut from pizza and soggy potatoes. There were canary faces and groundhog faces and faces of water buffalo. There were black eyes and rabbit eyes and noses made from dead vegetables and wet shoes and shopping bags.
—Edvins Beitiks, *San Francisco Examiner*

Observe a person. Use figurative comparisons to describe such features as his or her eyes, nose, skin, hair, voice, body type, and movement.

6. Connect People and Things

Try asking Barbara Walters–type questions: "If he were a tree, what kind of tree would he be?" Or building? Or wine? Or car model?

Match the person to their non-human representation:

Non-human representations
1. If _____ were a drink, he/she would be tap water.
2. If _____ were an element, he/she would be mercury.
3. If _____ were an automobile, he/she would be a Jaguar.
4. If _____ were a sea creature, he/she would be a dolphin.
5. If _____ were a food, he/she would be beef jerky.
6. If _____ were a dog, he/she would be a beagle.

Persons
a. Jimmy Stewart
b. Dan Quayle
c. Princess Diana
d. Madonna
e. Arnold Schwarzenegger
f. Joe Montana

Possible Answers: (1) b, (2) d, (3) c, (4) f, (5) e, (6) a

Here is an example of the way this kind of comparison can be used in writing. Anna Quindlen describes her father:

He has a personality, which, couched in culinary terms, would be something like clam chowder—the kind with the tomatoes, not the cream, the kind that seems to have odd little bits of everything thrown together, with a good deal of pepper. He is eccentric and

smart. When I was a small girl, my father used to take me, long past my bedtime, to a place called Joe's Bar and Grill, where it was so dark you couldn't see the pizza you were eating.

He gave me "The Many Loves of Dobie Gillis" after he had finished reading it himself. He danced the twist for our first dance at my wedding. He is no one's idea of the all-American father, no Ward Cleaver or Jimmy Stewart. Jimmy Cagney maybe.

He is not milk. My mother was milk; my father is clam chowder.

Consider someone you know well. Associate him or her with something that catches the person's essence. Explain the connection.

7. Make a Concept into a Person

You can bring an abstraction to life by giving it human qualities. The following sentences turn an idea into a human being, revealing its identity only at the end.

> *I am a born rebel. I reek with sedition and shake my fist at constituted authority. During my lifetime I have had only a single job: to guarantee the freedom to the American people. I am The Bill of Rights.* —Frank J Cobb, *LaFolette's Magazine* (1920)

> *My kingdom is as wide as the universe and my wants have no limits. I go forward always, freeing spirits and weighing worlds, without fear, without compassion, without love, without God. I am called Science.* —Gustave Flaubert

Use these models to give some of the following concepts human qualities:

▪ Ambition	▪ Trust	▪ Leadership	▪ Authority
▪ Censorship	▪ Curiosity	▪ Democracy	▪ Knowledge
▪ Compromise	▪ Wisdom	▪ Fate	▪ Justice
▪ Hope	▪ Faith	▪ Memory	▪ Humor
▪ Fame	▪ Guilt	▪ Hypocrisy	▪ Public Opinion
▪ Respect	▪ Idealism	▪ Progress	▪ Time
▪ Mediocrity	▪ Freedom	▪ Duty	▪ Reputation

Comment

Students can also try a third-person character sketch of a quality, as in the following example:

Example: Frugality

> *Frugality wakes to the sound of chirping birds, saving money on both an alarm clock and the electricity necessary to run it. Putting on the hand-me-down robe from her sister, Generosity, Frugal-*

ity washes her face and brushes her teeth with the dew collected from trees. Using a screwdriver, she squeezes the last ounce of toothpaste out of her flattened toothpaste container. Tiptoeing across her lawn to her sleeping neighbor's porch, she borrows his daily newspaper. She pops a two-day-old croissant into the microwave for one minute after which it will taste just like a fresh croissant. Unpeeling the packet of instant coffee she got at her doctor's office, she boils herself a cup of coffee, black because those little complimentary cream packs don't keep. Bringing her breakfast to the dining table, she unwraps the newspaper. With a public school issued pair of scissors, she cuts out the coupons and free sample offers, then neatly rewraps the paper and returns it to her neighbor's doorstep.

—Dylan Lee, age seventeen

Here are a some personal qualities that have inspired strong personified character studies: Self-Pity, Envy, Modesty, Flirtation, Caution, Perfection, Greed, Worry, Innocence, Ambivalence, and Boredom.

8. Create Analogies to Explain Big Ideas

Try turning abstract concepts into analogous specific narratives and descriptions.

> *Civilization is a stream with banks. The stream is sometimes filled with blood from people killing, stealing, shouting, and doing things historians usually record, while on the banks, unnoticed people build homes, make love, raise children, sing songs, write poetry, and even whittle statues.*
>
> *The story of civilization is the story of what happened on the banks. Historians are pessimists because they ignore the banks for the river.*
>
> —Will and Ariel Durant, *The Story of Civilization*

> *We—the entire human race—are standing on a subway platform. . . . On one side of the platform, the trains run one way. On the other side, they run in the opposite direction. It's a particularly creepy subway platform. There are no signs. Not above the tracks, not on the trains. And even if there were signs, the lighting is so bad that no one could read them. There is no way to tell which train is which. One pulls into the station. The doors open. We get on it. Moving—even if we don't know where we're going—is better than standing still. Sooner or later, we get the idea that we're going in the wrong direction. We get off the train at the next station, also dimly lit and lacking signs. We cross the platform and we go back the other way. We do this for all eternity. More or less. This is history.*
>
> —Karrie Jacobs, *Metropolis Magazine*

Or, less seriously: *Life is rather like a can of sardines—we're all looking for the key. . . . We roll back the lid of the sardine tin of life, we reveal the sardines, the riches of life therein, and we get them out, we enjoy them. But you know, there's always a little piece*

in the corner you can't get out. I wonder if there's a little piece in the
corner of your life? I know there is in mine.
  —Alan Bennett, *Beyond the Fringe*

These writers use analogies to make vivid large ideas about civilization, history, and the human condition. Can you develop an analogy to explain an equally large concept? Try comparing life to one of the following: a detective story, a Greek tragedy, an Elizabethan tragedy, a TV sit-com, a game (focus on a specific sport or game), a fairy tale, high school, a weekend in Las Vegas, a year of seasons, a trip to Disneyland, a prison, war, a game show, a novel or play by (choose an author), a voyage on a cruise ship, Christmas, or a business.

Choose one of these or one of your own. Then develop the details of the comparison.

Look! Up in the Sky. Is That a Rain Cloud or a Chunk of Dirty Cotton? Student Responses to Analogies

WRITING teachers learn pretty quickly that students don't all have the same capacity for creating, interpreting, and tolerating metaphors. In this, they are no different from the rest of us.

The student responses to the following statement by Malcolm X document both the power and danger of metaphor. Malcolm intended this analogy as a comment on white liberals.

> *A man who tosses worms in the river isn't necessarily a friend to the fish. All the fish who take him for a friend, who think that worm has got no hook on it, usually end up in the frying pan.*

What follows are three very different directions students took in interpreting Malcolm.

> *If my friend Jeremy had known about these words he might not have ended up in the "frying pan." He was a star pitcher for his high school (not this one) and a lot of scouts were trying to recruit him. One college arranged a trip to its campus. Jeremy flew first class and he said he was served some champagne on the flight. Nobody was even carding him even though he was seventeen at the time. They gave him their best room in a certain fancy dorm they keep for stuff like this and talked to him about what a great deal they were going to give him if he went to their school. I think you could say they "tossed him a lot of worms." When he came back he showed pictures of himself surrounded by a lot of girls at a party.*
>
> *But when he actually went to the school, he started to realize there was a "hook" attached to the deal. In college, he had to read quite a few books every week and he had never been very interested in reading. He*

had to practice baseball all the time too. Whereas, in high school he just had to do his homework and didn't have to read much.

To make a long story short, he started to realize that those who tossed him a worm in the river weren't necessarily his friends, but were just interested in his pitching. He dropped out of this big school and now he goes to a junior college where he's working on his reading and writing skills. He says he may play ball again later.

—Victor, grade eleven

There are many things wrong with this quotation. First of all, nobody ever just throws worms in a river. People who like to feed animals feed ducks or pigeons or if there is a zoo around they will go to give peanuts to the monkeys. Only a crazy person would feed fish worms with no hooks. Also fish don't have "friends," and if they did they would probably be other fish, not humans.

—Helene, grade eleven

This analogy gets at a common phenomena: the tendency of naive people to accept any act of friendliness without taking into consideration who is offering it or the fact that the "bait" may be attached to a "hook," or that jumping at the "worm" may bring unpleasant consequences. Malcolm X meant this analogy to apply to race relations but it can also apply to people in other types of situations. The "worm" may be a credit card and the "fish" a young person living on a budget. Or the "friend" might me a politician throwing out all kinds of promises which are going to cost everyone, including "the fish," higher taxes later. You could say the moral of this is "the early fish should avoid the worm."

—Dennis, grade twelve

9. Know When to Explain a Comparison

You can use a simile as a starting place for an explanation.

The Democratic [party] *debates* [in 1988] *have been like the mating of pandas in the zoo.* (**Explanation**) *Expectations are high, there's a lot of fuss and commotion, but there's never any kind of result.* —Bruce Babbitt, then a Democratic presidential candidate.

Money is like manure. (**Explanation**) *If you spread it around it does a lot of good, but if you pile it up in one place it stinks like hell.* —Clint Murchinson, Texas oilman

Being in politics is like being a football coach. (**Explanation**) *You have to be smart enough to understand the game, and dumb enough to think it's important.* —Eugene McCarthy, former U.S. senator

Pick some of the following comparisons you believe might benefit from a sentence of explanation. Write a sentence or two which connects the figurative to the literal.

- *Music is easy; acting is like having the party at your house; singing is like going to someone else's.* —Cher

- *Revolutions are like the most noxious dunghills which bring into life the noblest vegetables.* —Napoleon Bonaparte

- *Religion . . . is the opium of the people.* —Karl Marx

- A critic quotes a Yiddish proverb in responding to the statement of a young a movie star's claim that Shakespeare is "irrelevant today." The proverb: *The girl who can't dance says the band can't play.*

- On the aches, pains, and minor illnesses of old age: *When a man expects to be arrested, every knock on the door is an alarm.* —Sidney Smith

- On fate: *As yet the hounds are still playing in the courtyard, but their prey will not escape, however fast it may already be charging through the forest.* —Franz Kafka

- A disgruntled car owner asks a consumer affairs reporter if she should address her complaints to the customer relations department of the auto manufacturer or go to the head of the company. The reporter answers: *There is no reason to attack the monkey when the organ grinder is present.*

Fun and Games for Serious Writers: Seven Ways to Play with Words

1. Make Up New Words

Don't be shy about inventing a new word. You won't be alone. Every day since 1966, an average of six new words have been added to the English language. Many of them have stuck. "Foodie," "ghetto blaster," and "leg warmer" are recorded in dictionaries.

Three techniques for inventing new words:

Make allusions

- People keenly aware of everything going on around them become *Janusians* after the Roman two-faced god who could look in two directions at once.
- In the movie *Clueless,* one teenage character says that another is a "total *Monet,*" that is, like the works of the artist Monet, this girl looks terrific until you get up close.

Combine existing words

- A company calls a layoff to achieve greater efficiency in a depressed market *rightsizing.*
- Walter Winchell combined two words to describe a happy event: the couple was *infanticipating.*

Combine prefixes and suffixes

- A *nonist* is a health freak who goes so far as to abstain from all substances and activities that could even remotely harm his or her health.
- *Psychotronic* describes a film genre which includes the subcategories horror, fantasy and science fiction.

Think of a phenomenon which has gone unnamed—an awkward pause in conversation, a tedious text required for a course, the ritual waiters go through when they recite the specials of the day. Find a word for that which is previously unnamed.

New words are most useful when they help you say something you really want to say. Try integrating your new word in a paragraph:

> *I am not up to the rigors of trying on new clothes. It's no use blaming anyone but me. Not only am I incapable of quick changes, I also suffer from what has been diagnosed as severe **ensembleosis**, or dread of clashing colors, the paralyzing inability to decide between a brown tie with dots and a brown tie without dots.*
> —Gerald Nachman, *San Francisco Chronicle*

2. Try Punning

If you have a talent for puns, use it. Try out words which can be taken in two senses or have the similar sound of a different word. Stay away from the obvious (BARE FACTS PRESENTED AT NUDE BEACH HEARING). And from the corny and pointless. ("I tried to telephone the zoo this morning, but the lion was busy.") Here are some classy models, beginning with Shakespeare, the acknowledged champion of English language punsters:

- Lord Chief Justice (to the fat and profligate Falstaff): *Your means are very slender and your waste great.*
  Falstaff: *I would that my means were greater and my waist slenderer.*
- What did Martina Navratilova ask the State Department when she defected to the United States? *Do you cache Czechs here?*
- *Parking is such street sorrow.* —Herb Caen
- The lead on a news story reporting on the prison murder of Richard Loeb (of the homicidal duo Leopold and Loeb) after Loeb had made sexual advances towards another inmate: *Richard Loeb, a college educated man who should have known better, has ended his sentence with a proposition.*
- *Do television evangelists do more than lay people?*—Stanley Ralph Ross
- Christmas-time ad line for Stetson hats many years ago: *Make Your Presents Felt.*
- Billboard ad shows bowl of cottage cheese. Caption: *Skinny dip*

Three drama reviews:

- A negative review of the play, "I Am a Camera": *Me No Leica.*
- A headline on review of a production of Shakespeare's most famous play in which the title character had performed drunk: *Ham Lit.*
- A review of an actor's insecure performance as King Lear: *He*

*played the king under the apprehension that at any moment some-
one was going to play the ace.*

One way to practice puns is to create some punny store names:

- A shop in Los Angeles selling clothes previously used in the
  movies: "A Star Has Worn"
- A San Francisco coffee shop: "Espresso Yourself"

Or try thinking of punny business names that could be connected
to streets in your town.

Student examples for San Francisco streets:

- Laundromat on Eureka Street: *Eureka Not* (Ryan Shankel)
- Paranormal novelty story on Lake Street: *Lake Eerie* (Laura
  Maloney)
- Large woman's clothing store on Broadway: *Big Broad Ways*
  (Priscilla Fong)
- Futon shop on Lyon Street: *Take It Lyon Down* (Renee Mo)
- Pancake restaurant on Hayes Street: *Hayes Stacks* (Michael
  Chee)

Comment

These student examples make no pretense at Shakespearean cleverness, but by beginning with street names, I give students who have
never before made an intentional pun a place to start. I like to pass out
maps so as to provide the additional benefit of a local geography lesson.

---

3. Indulge in a Little Alliteration

You can get attention with alliterative sentences that repeat beginning word sounds. Done right, you can create a pleasant buzz as Shakespeare knew when he wrote in *Antony and Cleopatra:*

How sweet the moonlight sleeps upon this bank!
Here we will sit and let the sounds of music
Creep in our ears; soft stillness and the night
Become the touches of sweet harmony.

Rather than something like:

How sweet the moonlight lies upon this bank!
Here we will be and let the tones of music
Creep in our ears; faint quiet and the night
Become the touches of fine harmony.

Keep an ear out for the possibility of introducing subtle and occasional alliterations. Getting the right sound balance is a tricky skill. Change the phrase "a collection of buzzwords" to "a bunch of buzzwords" and you are dangerously close to a "Peter Piper picked a peck … " exaggerated repetition, but make it "bouillabaisse of buzzwords" and you've added an effective zing.

Make some one-sentence statements promoting a cause in which you believe. Then revise them, trying for some alliteration which is subtle, not overbearing. Phrases like "nattering nabobs of negativism" or "pusillanimous pussyfooters" favored by a former vice-president are memorable but too strong for everyday consumption. Go for the less obvious. Remember that in a first draft, "These are the times that try men's souls" could have been, "During the 1770s, we are all facing challenges which test our character."

Can you do as well altering, say, "Money spent on the infrastructure can improve the economy and pull us together as a nation?"

4. Alter a Cliché

With a little ingenuity, you can turn a hackneyed phrase into an original statement. Here are some models:

- *There's a deception to every rule.* —Hal Lee Luyah
- *Truth is more of a stranger than fiction.* —Mark Twain
- *I am two with nature.* —Woody Allen
- *Time wounds all heels.* —Groucho Marx
- *Work is the curse of the drinking classes.* —Anonymous
- *I'm as pure as the driven slush.* —Talulah Bankhead
- *Where there's a will there's a lawsuit.* —Addison Mizzen
- *There's been a lot of Perrier under the bridge since 1968.* —Linda Ellerbee
- *A thing of beauty is a joy for a while.* —Hal Lee Luyah

Try altering some clichés. Here are some common expressions that might inspire you:

- one foot in the grave
- the blind leading the blind
- a fate worse than death
- knocked over with a feather
- wouldn't touch it with a ten-foot pole
- a man after my own heart
- when all is said and done
- burn the candle at both ends
- jump from the frying pan into the fire
- grin and bear it
- keep a stiff upper lip
- live and let live
- look for a needle in a haystack
- be on pins and needles
- put all your eggs in one basket

- risk life and limb
- sell like hot cakes
- have your cake and eat it too
- cry over spilt milk
- escape by the skin of your teeth
- take the bull by the horns
- vanish into thin air

Put your phrase in the context of a paragraph to make clearer the phrase's meaning and your intention.

Student Example: One foot in the grave

> *About six months ago techno-music was starting to take over my life. No doubt about it, **I had one foot in the raves**. I lived for one o'clock in the morning when I would sneak out of the house in my Cat in the Hat outfit and drive with my friends to a South of Market Warehouse where I'd spend the night blowing whistles. I'd get all fueled up on "healthy" smart drinks and gyrate until dawn to the pulse of the drum machine. Those were the good times before my 2.3 grade point average brought me back to the real world.*

5. Make Up Jokes

As almost all humor is specific, you can practice being specific by making up jokes. Here's how:

Take a sheet of paper. Draw a line down the middle. Pick a noun like "car." Fill the left hand column with things you associate with car (keep the nouns singular; plurals usually don't make specific pictures): mechanic, windshield wiper, bumper, ashtray, traffic jam, flat tire, parking control officer, back seat, dashboard clock, trunk.

Then pick a trait such as "old" or "ancient." In the right hand column list specifics associated with this adjective: caveman, Garden of Eden, fossil, liver spots, George Burns, Medicare, wheelchair, sundial.

Then mix the two to see what you will come up with:

- My car is so old it has liver spots.
- My car is so old it has a bumper sticker that says "Garden of Eden: Love It or Leave It."
- My car is so old it has a sundial instead of a clock.*

Try this exercise. Even if your jokes are not all that funny, remember you are training yourself to be specific.

(*Based on the technique of comedy teacher John Cantu reported by Michael Robertson, *San Francisco Chronicle*.)

6. Play with Definitions

Sometimes you can clarify your opinion by creating a definition which is a form of editorial comment. Focus on a word about which you have an opinion. Put the word in a category or class. Add your own defining characteristics:

- *fashion:* a despot (class) whom the wise ridicule and obey (characteristics) —Ambrose Bierce

- *happiness:* an imaginary condition (class) formerly attributed by the living to the dead, now usually attributed by adults to children, and by children to adults (characteristics) —Thomas Szasz

- *motorcycling:* a form of transportation (class) most appropriate for those who believe that gas, vehicle maintenance, and life itself should be cheap (characteristics)

- *camera:* a mechanical device for recording images (class) activated when pointed in the general direction of a blinking human (characteristic)

- *aerobic exercise class:* near-death experience (class) which, unlike other such experiences, substitutes heavy bass disco for the Music of the Spheres and fluorescent light for the soft, ethereal kind (characteristics)

- *stress:* all-purpose excuse (class) which permits activity as varied as staying in bed on a workday with the covers pulled over your head to throwing a tantrum when you finally decide to get up (characteristics)

7. Juggle Parts of Speech

Try turning a word normally used as a noun or an adjective into a verb. This device has been around at least as long as Shakespeare:

- Cleopatra: *He **words** me, girls, he **words** me.*
- Shylock: ***Foot** me as you spurn a stranger cur.*

More recent examples:

- Health advice from legendary pitcher Satchell Paige: *Avoid fried meats which **angry** up the blood.*
- A government official testifies at the Iran-Contra hearings, claiming he wasn't paying attention to day-to-day details: *I didn't **flyspeck** them.*
- A San Francisco bike messenger describes a close call he had with a driver who was getting out of a car: *Some guy almost **doored** me today. I thought I was going to die.*

The more concrete the noun or adjective, the more appropriate the transformation to a verb. Abstract nouns converted to verbs—"prioritize," "optimize," "reincentivize," or "problematize"—ring of bureaucracy, sound ugly, and make no pictures.

Write some sentences in which you convert some specific nouns or adjectives to verbs.

Comment

Another way to juggle parts of speech is to convert nouns to hyphenated adjectives:

Letter to the Editor:
> *(Kitty) Kelly's book represents the public's revenge for the **spoon-fed, spin-controlled, photo-opted, sound-bitten** image the Reagans issued America.*"—Adair Rowland, *Newsweek*

Verbal Aerobics: The Advanced Course

FOR those seeking a more vigorous language workout, here are additional exercises.

1. **Create an acronym.** An acronym is a word, the letters of which stand for other words. (SCUBA: Self-Contained Underwater Breathing Apparatus.) It might work best to start with a recognized word and make each letter stand for a relevant word. For example:

   PROM: *Presumptuous Ritual Ordering (a) Manhunt* —Natasha Zaretsky, age seventeen

   LOWRIDERS: *Latinos on Wheels Really Into Driving Everywhere Real Slow* —Bo Joseph, age seventeen

2. **Make up ten appropriate proper names for individual members of a class or species.**

   Trees: *Elmer, Pineton, Barkman, Twiggie, Leafy, Woody, Stub, Stumper, Woodstalk, Oakley* —Ken Skidmore, age seventeen

3. **Create a set of numbers to replace the mundane one to ten. The set should link together in some way.**

   a, whop, bobba, loo, bob, awhop, bam, boom, tutti, fruitti —Ruben O'Malley, age eighteen

   olive, twist, tuaca, fizz, frangelica, shot, smooth, ernest, nada, tequila —Ericka Gettman, age eighteen

4. **Create an anagram using the letters of the name of a well-known person. The new configuration should make a comment on the person's role or character.**

Clint Eastwood: *Old West Action* —Vanessa Misler, age seventeen

Oliver "Ollie" North: *Li'l Hero, evil or not*—Junna Ro, age eighteen

5. **Try a gradatio.** A gradatio uses the object of one clause or phrase as the subject of the next to tell a story or make a comment.

   Classic example: *The boy is the most powerful of all the Hellenes; for the Hellenes are commanded by the Athenians, the Athenians by myself, myself by the boy's mother, and the mother by her boy.* —Thenistocles

   Or this anonymous graffiti (which cheats a little on the form): *God is love. Love is blind. Ray Charles is blind. Therefore, Ray Charles is God.*

   Student example: *All of my worrying causes me stress; my stress causes me to eat; eating cause me to break out; breaking out causes me to worry.* —Erin Jones, age sixteen

6. **Write a homophone headline and tell the story.** A homophone is a word that is pronounced like another word but is different in meaning or spelling. These words cause problems even for experienced writers in a hurry, as in this headline during the 1984 Presidential campaign.

   juggler/jugular: REAGAN GOES FOR THE JUGGLER IN THE MIDWEST

   bore/boar (student example): GOLDEN GATE PARK SCENE OF ASSAULTS BY WILD BORES

Visitors to Golden Gate Park in recent weeks have been approached by an elderly couple who introduce themselves as "Jane and Ward." They approach their victims under the pretense they are fellow picnickers who have run out of hot dog buns. Police report that the couple will strike up a conversation about the weather and then without warning whip out photo albums, letters, paintings, drawings, scrap books and recordings all done by their grandchildren. Victims say that the couple becomes increasingly wild and crazy as they warm to, what one listener called, "a very boring story." —Akane Saunders, age seventeen

7. **Play with place names.** Suppose the names of cities and towns were used to give names to people, things thoughts or events that have no name. A Webster could be a device for dislodging spiders.

Student examples:

Petaluma: *organization dedicated to encouraging physical attention to the small rodent called a luma* —Daniel Handler, age seventeen

Yosemite: *greeting directed toward a Black Hebrew* —Princeton Chan, age seventeen

Soledad: *new word for a single father* —Erin Weiser, age seventeen

8. **Play the horizontal-vertical game.** Spell out vertically a quality, such as "obedience," "stubbornness," or "patience." Use each letter of the word as the first letter in a phrase which illustrates that quality.

Student example:

Picking up after four young children
Aiding a ninety-year-old on a five-mile walk
Trying to put together a five thousand piece puzzle
Inching one's way to perfection
Expecting world peace
Netting fish without bait
Completing twenty years of school to become a doctor
Experiencing pleasure in watching a tree grow
        —Cate Corcoran, age eighteen

9. **Create some new collective nouns.** We have a *coven* of witches, a *kindle* of kittens, a *clowder* of cats. What else?

   a swelling of pregnant moms —Lesley Aiken, age seventeen
   a grinning of game show hosts —Odetta Ogletree, age
        eighteen
   a clutching of kleptomaniacs —Megan Jones, age seventeen
   a woofing of weavers —Lara Sao Pedro, age seventeen
   a wave of surfers —Vanessa Misler, age seventeen
   a spattering of abstract expressionists —Bernadine Mellis, age
        eighteen

10. **Play at cliché-aversion therapy.** This last bit of verbal gymnastics demands that those who try it have an overstocked storehouse of clichés. Cliché aversion therapy works like chocolate aversion therapy, the attempt to cure a chocolate addiction by marathon gorging on mousses and bon bons.

   This game applies this principle to those who have a sweet tooth for clichés.

One of the players introduces a cliché. The second player responds with a cliché that contains one of the words in the original cliché (excluding prepositions and articles).

First player: Truth will out.

Second player: Out of the frying pan into the fire.

First player: Baptism by fire.

The round continues until one of the players can't respond. Players can start with the following words that are heavily used in common expressions:

death (dead), change, black, beauty, blind, blood, blessing, hand, eye, born, burn, cat, dog, cold, cry, easy, eat, fall, first, gift, head, keep, last, man, name, old, pay, put, read, see, time, take, hope, wet, young, fair

Cliché aversion therapy works particularly well as a team game. And, of course, for many students the purpose of the game may not be "aversion" at all but rather sharing and increasing their knowledge of common idioms.

Part VII: Writers Keep Trying

- Once More from the Top:
  Four Ways to Revise Your Writing

Back to the Drawing Board:
The Why and How of Revision

I am sitting at a meeting of the San Francisco Planning Commission, listening to the commissioners respond to the plans of a condominium developer and his architect. The applicants are told they are going to need to make a few changes in their plan. Again. This will be the third revision. The commissioners *do* find some nice things to say about the project: the developers are to be commended for planning to replace the unsightly shacks now on this property. But the commissioners have some ideas to improve the architect's work. Why not add more decorative features and more setbacks? Why not reduce the number of units to cut back on the bulk? Wouldn't another type of landscaping be more appropriate? The architect is accepting these suggestions with a seasoned composure. He tells the commissioners that he will return in a month with revised plans.

I am thinking I have watched something close to this process hundreds of times. In English class, we do not have architects and planning commissions, but we do have writers and response groups. The responders are not seated on an elevated dais, and they are expected to give more support than the rather grudging praise the commissioners allow this project. Further, the writer seldom accepts criticism as coolly as the architect absorbs these swipes at his best effort. Seventeen-year-olds are not yet experts at taking the knocks and disguising the hurt.

But the questions the commissioners ask this builder are the questions that response groups learn to ask writers and writers learn to ask themselves: What works best here and, therefore, should be highlighted? What needs to be added? Removed? Altered? Why? Not only writers and architects, but all creative people, trying to do work which is more than slapdash and superficial, ask these questions. The writing response group can provide the training wheels for writers developing these self-critical habits.

I am, of course, presenting a neat overview of a messy process. I have seen students turn their desks toward the wall, upset by a rudely phrased critique or by the general "dorkiness" of their associates. I have overheard shocking details of weekend parties exchanged when students appeared to be in animated conversation about a Problem-Solution paper. I have listened while students who think they already know the answer ask me, "How come you're making us do your job fixing up these papers?"

Putting aside the "When did you stop beating your wife?" insinuations built into this question, I try to respond. I am asking them to work together to "fix up" their writing so that when they leave my class they will take with them a friendly but persistent inner voice that gives them the courage and discipline to look again at what they have written. The voice will ask, "What should I add? What should I take out? What should I change and why?" The challenges in this section allow students to think about these "Whats" and "Whys" but also give some clues as to the "Hows."

While these few workouts touch on some specific skills relevant for revision, in fact, writers should draw on all the challenges in this book whenever they look again at their drafts.

As they become more fluent writers, they will see that writing it down is sometimes the easy part. Often the more difficult, creative and satisfying part comes with looking out the window, mulling over the possibilities for change.

Once More from the Top:
Four Ways to Revise Your Writing

1. Revise for Specifics

A first draft is often full of ideas and short on specifics. You can alter this imbalance in two ways: (1) augment general statements with specific examples, (2) convert some general statements to more specific ones. Here's some practice with both techniques.

(1) In the following paragraph, add a clause or sentence of vivid examples to support each general statement.

> *While few people find their sixtieth birthday an occasion to stand up and cheer, many who reach that age take comfort in the wisdom that comes with experience. They have experienced adolescence, a painful period of physical and emotional change. This was a time* **when each new zit seemed to have the impact of an erupting volcano.** *They've spent their twenties struggling for an education or taking orders on a new job* _____ .
> *By their thirties many faced the responsibilities of marriage and family* _____ . *At the same time they were competing for promotions on the job. In their forties and fifties they lived through the so-called mid-life crisis* _____ .
> *Further, these were the years they felt the burden of guiding their children through their difficult teens* _____ .
> *But by sixty, some people, at least, are retired and others are financially secure* _____ . *If they are among the lucky ones, they may now relax and enjoy life.*

(2) In the following paragraph, replace the bolded general statements with vivid detail. For instance, the clause, "She can get up when she wants to" could become, "Alarm clocks are no longer part of her life."

A famous artist has complete control over her life. **She can get up when she wants to and eat whatever she wants for breakfast. She can practice her art for awhile, go places with people, or do unusual things alone. She can accept or reject anyone she meets. She can dress any way she wants and spend money on impractical things.** *She can do all these things as long as she continues to create expensive and sought-after paintings.*

2. Revise for Consistent Tone and Details

Don't intrude on a light-hearted piece of writing with a dollop of gloom; don't interrupt general advice with a picayune prescription. If you have decided to be serious, stay sober. If you are just fooling around, keep joking.

Two examples of inconsistent tone—one intentional, one not:

> A comedian tells his audience: *Whew, I'm having a rough day. Woke up this morning late, missed the bus. I was so backed up, I had to work through the lunch hour. Then later on I found out I had cancer.*

> Vanna White gives her philosophy of life: *Be happy. Stay healthy. Feel good. Stay in shape. Treat others like you want others to treat you. Keep moisturizer on your face.*

Find details in the following student paragraph which seem out of place. Explain why:

> *The requirement that we must take art for graduation is ridiculous. Why should a person who can't draw a straight line and has no desire to learn to do it have her grade point destroyed by some people on the board of education who think everyone should be "well-rounded" or whatever. It seems like they just keep loading stuff on us: more required English, computer literacy, AIDS awareness, twenty cents more than it used to be to buy a hot dog at the snack bar, voter education lessons, and taking graduation pictures right after gym class when your hair could be wet from having a shower.*

List items relevant to one or more of the following topics. Decide if you want your reasons to be serious or humorous, general or specific. Keep your word choices consistent with this decision.

- Ways to tell the romance is over

- Ways shopping malls have improved the quality of American life or detracted from it

- Ways to get free publicity for a cause

- Advantages of a large family (or disadvantages)

- Life lessons which can be learned taking public transportation

- Things you would not know if you had never watched Saturday morning kids' TV

Comment

Sometimes, of course, writers make creative use of discontinuity:

Mixing little stuff and big stuff: *The way you hold your knife/ The way you sip your tea/ The way your changed my life/ No, they can't take that away from me.*
—Ira Gershwin

Mixing pompous language and slangy language: *Everyone, in some small sacred sanctuary of the self, is nuts.*
—Leo Rosten

---

3. Revise for Simple, Direct Statements

If you don't need a word, don't use it. Profound ideas can be simply stated. The Lord's Prayer has 56 words, the Gettysburg Address, 266 words, the Ten Commandments, 297 words.

Economy of language is one sign that you know what you are talking about.

Apply the calling card test:

If you can't write your idea on the back of my calling card, you don't have a clear idea. —David Belasco

Study these varied statements, none of which waste words:

The enemy advances; we retreat. The enemy halts; we harass. The enemy tires; we attack. The enemy retreats; we pursue. —Mao Zedong

The right of the police of Boston to affiliate, which has always been questioned, never granted, is now prohibited. There is no right to strike against the public safety by anybody, anywhere, anytime. —Massachusetts Governor Calvin Coolidge, 1919

Congress shall make no law respecting an establishment of religion, or prohibiting the free exercise thereof; or abridging the freedom of speech, or the press; or the right of the people to peaceably assemble, and to petition the government for a redress of grievances. —James Madison, First Amendment to the U.S. Constitution

To spend too much time in studies is sloth; to use them too much for ornament, is affectation; to make judgment wholly by their rules is the humor of a scholar. ... Read not to contradict and confute; nor to believe and take for granted; nor to find

talk and discourse; but to weigh and consider. Some books are to be tasted, other to be swallowed, and some few to be chewed and digested. —Francis Bacon, "Of Studies"

From a small town newspaper "crime report": *Guerneville— Besotted mendicant who was urinating in public was arrested for all of those things.*

General McAuliffee replies to a demand that he surrender, Battle of the Bulge, 1944: *Nuts.*

Text of the telegram Victor Hugo sent to his publisher upon the publication of *Les Miserables:* "*?*"
His publisher's answer: "*!*"
The first edition had sold out within twenty-four hours.

Using no more than thirty-five words, make a clear, accurate and complete statement of some practical idea or moral concept which directs your life. Don't rush. "If I had more time I would write a shorter letter," wrote Blaise Pascal, French philosopher.

Word Surgery: How to Take a Scalpel to Flabby Language

I want to convince students that one of the great joys of revision is crossing out words, watching their prose grow muscular as they destroy empty unproductive phrases.

Here's one way I do this. I provide each student with that ultimate symbol of teacher power, a red pen. (I've used pencils but somehow they come off as pale, unconvincing substitutes.) Then I ask students to confront paragraphs such as the ones below, imagining they are plastic surgeons of language slicing away at the cellulose of flabby prose. As they get into this, an aura of good feeling comes to dominate the classroom, as if by eliminating these language excesses students are performing a public good, the same feeling they may have had on the Earth Day field trip as they cleaned up the trash-infested picnic area.

After students remove the flab, I encourage them to restructure the sentences. Students can keep the language they root out from these paragraphs. The words will serve them as a beginner's glossary of garbage language.

The paragraphs:

In our society it seems to me there is definitely too dominant a level of sex and violence in the field of entertainment. This is because of the fact that, for the people who make movies, TV shows and recordings, the purpose of this mass media is to make money. It stands to reason, therefore, that, by and large, there is a tendency to put out work that is, frankly speaking, very tasteless but which actually makes lots of money.

It should be noted that even though the level of complaint about this type of media is high, the primary contributing factor to the existence of these works—so far as experts who know are concerned—is that the public, in general, has thus far been very eager to buy anything along the lines of entertainment filled with violence and pornography.

To emphasize the importance of this last point I want to conclude by quoting Pogo who said something very much worth listening to in the following words: "We have met the enemy and he is us." With reference to the kind of thing I have been saying above it appears that Pogo was right.

One lean and restructured version:

Because most people who make movies, recordings, and TV shows are in it for the money, works which contain excessive sex and violence—but also make big profits—dominate our mass media.

One reason for this dominance is that, while many complain about these works, much of the public eagerly buys sexually explicit and violent entertainment. As Pogo said, "We have met the enemy and he is us."

4. Revise for Conciseness

Learn to say more in fewer words by practicing the one-sentence plot overview.

Here are some models from those who make a profession of saying a lot about a story in a few words.

Rosemary's Baby: *Rosemary's actor-husband conspires with a coven, drugs her and mates her with Satan in exchange for a Broadway hit…* —Pauline Kael

Casablanca: *Everything is right in this WW2 classic of war-torn Casablanca with elusive nightclub owner Rick (Bogart) finding old flame (Bergman) and her husband, underground leader (Henried), among skeletons in his closet.* —Leonard Maltin

The Graduate: *An unforgettable, touching, funny, unsettling film about a young man (Dustin Hoffman) who, as he attempts to chart his future and develop his own set of values, falls in love with Katherine Ross, but finds himself seduced by Ann Bancroft, her wily, sexy mother.* —Mick Martin and Marsha Palmer, *Video Movie Guide*

Dr. Strangelove: *(This is an unlikely comedy in which) a Strategic Air Command General orders bomb-carrying planes under his command to attack Russia, touching off a series of hectic, exciting events in settings alternating between the base, commanded by the general who started it all, the plane en route to the U.S.S.R. and the Pentagon's War Room where the Chief Executive is trying to head off Nuclear War.* —Variety Movie Guide

Try a one sentence plot overview of a favorite film.

Essay

Hello. Operator. Get Me Group Response: The Nitty Gritty of Group Revision

HOW can we encourage students to be active editors of each others' work? I can only provide pieces of an answer, footnotes to those books that take up this question in detail. Here are some principles I have learned the hard way.

1. Everyone needs to know the task: to identify the paper's strengths and to improve the paper by suggesting additions, deletions and alterations. The more familiar students are with the concepts in these workouts, the more effectively they will be able to work together toward this end.

2. The quality of response improves dramatically when every student in the group has a copy of the work under consideration. I learned this during the brief period before the vice-principal started to write me nasty notes about overusing the Xerox machine.

3. Each work should be read aloud by at least two readers: the writer and one other person in the group. Readers and listeners should note places that the reader slows down, a good sign that some syntactical knots need to be untangled. Listeners also should be aware of places they have a strong desire to tune out, another indication that they have come on a passage that needs revision.

4. Editors and writers should, of course, talk about the piece, and all editors should be expected to say something about the work, but, additionally, editors should write out at least some of their suggestions so the entire conversation does not drift away on gossamer wing.

5. One thing a teacher can do to help the response process along is to be on the lookout for revision comments that are specific enough to be useful, but general enough so that the writer is left with alternative ways to make the revision. As she comes on these nuggets, she should share them with the class.

6. Writers should understand that revision suggestions, carefully considered, often suggest strong ideas that may never have occurred to the editors. (See, for example, the addition of "the girl in the window" in the model which follows.)

Model: What follows are two drafts of a paper by high school senior Holden Yu. Between the first and second draft are selected comments generated by his editing/response group. Your students can read the first draft, make their own suggestions, read the suggestions of the editors in the model and determine how these comments generated changes in the final draft.

No Title

One day a few years ago my mother and I were coming home on the bus together. She had been working and I had been in Marin hiking and having a good time. I was feeling guilty. My mother had always been selfless and caring. Someday I thought I would make it up to her.

As we got off the bus, I saw two kids walking behind us. We hastened our step and were half a block from home when I heard running. I turned around and I saw one teenager about thirty feet behind and another running past me toward my mother. She called out as one of the purse snatchers grabbed her purse. Her shopping bags were thrown on the ground during the struggle and her groceries spilled. Finally, the youth overpowered my mother, and she reluctantly released her hold on the purse. He ran off with the purse and his friend. Everything had happened too quickly for me to react.

Then I heard my mother say something. I thought she wanted me to go after them, but they were already half a block away. I started to shout for help, but not very loudly. I ran, but not as quickly as I should have. Fear held me back. I knew I was afraid of these kids. I became less determined in my pursuit, and soon they were a block ahead of me. They disappeared around the corner. I gave up and walked back. I had failed, not because I couldn't catch them, but because I wouldn't. I had just put on an act for my mother. As I approached her, I noticed her expression. I was prepared to tell her that her these boys had outrun me, hoping she wouldn't be too mad. But she wasn't angry.

Instead, she wanted to know why I had chased them at all. She said that I could have been hurt. I had not understood her words. I answered, "After what they did, how could I let them get away with it," fooling her but not myself. I know I did what I did because I was afraid of getting into trouble.

Editors' Comments

- The best part of this paper is that it is very honest. I admire the way you admit to being a coward. Maybe you could put even more of this in.
- Remember you should try to start with a picture or action. You don't do that. Maybe all through this you could explain more about how you are feeling.
- I think you need to get in more about how you are feeling.
- "I noticed her expression." What was her expression?
- Always try to be specific. How were you "having a good time in Marin?"
- How old were you when this occurred? I think that makes a big difference in what you did.
- Try to add more dialogue between you and your mom.
- You should add some stuff to give more of a picture of the neighborhood. Is anyone else around?

- Look at your verbs when the attack and chase are going on. Try to get more action in them.
- What did these kids look like?
- Try adding some specifics here and there. What was in the grocery bag, for instance?
- The words "hastened our steps" don't sound like the kind of words you use in the rest of the paper.

The Purse Which Spoke Truth

My mother was taking a nap on the bus. She was crouched in the corner of her seat against the window, tired from a hard day's work. I, on the other hand, had spent a carefree day, hiking and swimming in Marin, I was feeling guilty. My mother had always been a selfless and caring mother. Someday, I thought I, would make it up to her. Many times I had told her, "Mom, when I grow up, I'll buy you a Mercedes," but I had not yet shown my gratitude. As the bus approached our stop, I said to her, "Mom, one day I'll make you proud of me."

We got off and passed several children playing basketball on the sidewalk. Suddenly, as we passed a neighbor's house, I noticed that the neighbor's daughter had quickly left the window. Curious, I looked back, and I understood. The girl had seen two punks following us and she didn't want to get involved. We hurried along the block when suddenly one of the punks ran past me and towards my mother. She screamed as one of thugs grabbed her purse. Her shopping bags were thrown on the ground during the struggle; a bottle of soy sauce cracked on the sidewalk.

Meanwhile, I watched, still disbelieving. Then I heard my mother say something. I thought she wanted me to go after them, but I hesitated; they were half a block away before I pursued them. I ran, but not as quickly as I could have. I shouted, "Help, help," but not as loudly as I should have. Fear and selfishness held me back. I knew I really didn't want to catch these kids.

Even if I caught them, what could one thirteen-year-old boy do to two much older teenagers? Was the purse or the need to get revenge for my mother worth the risk of getting beaten up? I slowed down and soon they were a block ahead of me. They disappeared around a corner. I gave up and slowly walked back, my head hung in disappointment.

The girl at the window returned, looking down at the cowardly hypocrite. I had failed, not because I couldn't catch them, but because I wouldn't. My chase was just an act I had put on for my mother. As I approached her, I noticed her questioning expression. I was prepared to lie. I was going to tell her that her assailants outran me, hoping she wouldn't be mad. Ironically, she asked, "Why did you go after them? They might have hurt you." I had confused her words. She had said not "Chase them," but "Don't chase them."

I answered, "After what they did, how could I let them get away with it?" I was fooling her but not me. Deep down, I knew that I did what I did, not out of love but out of fear of being scolded.